Differentiating ^{K-2} Instruction
With Centers

in the Inclusive Classroom

Differentiating Instruction

K-2

With Centers

in the inclusive classroom

Judith Sower and Laverne Warner, Ph.D.

Prufrock Press Inc.

Waco, Texas

Library of Congress Cataloging-in-Publication Data

Sower, Judith, 1947-
 Differentiating instruction with centers in the inclusive classroom (K-2) / by Judith Sower and Laverne Warner.
    p. cm.
 Includes bibliographical references.
 ISBN 978-1-59363-715-6 (pbk.)
 1. Classroom learning centers. 2. Education, Primary. 3. Individualized instruction. 4. Mixed ability grouping in edu-
cation. I. Warner, Laverne, 1941- II. Title.
 LB3044.8.S67 2011
 371.2'52--dc23
                      2011016918

Edited by Lacy Compton

Cover and layout design by Raquel Trevino

ISBN-13: 978-1-59363-715-6

At the time of this book's publication, all facts and figures cited are the most current available. All telephone numbers, addresses, and websites URLs are accurate and active. All publications, organizations, websites, and other resources exist as described in the book, and all have been verified. The authors and Prufrock Press Inc. make no warranty or guarantee concerning the information and materials given out by organizations or content found at websites, and we are not responsible for any changes that occur after this book's publication. If you find an error, please contact Prufrock Press Inc.

Prufrock Press Inc.
P.O. Box 8813
Waco, TX 76714-8813
Phone: (800) 998-2208
Fax: (800) 240-0333
http://www.prufrock.com

DEDICATION

This book is dedicated to:
Joshua, Elizabeth, and Elijah Fuller;
Madeline Sower and Nicholas Conlee;
Delton Warner Phelps; and
Zoey Lauren and Molly Kate Hill.

ACKNOWLEDGMENTS

We would like to thank Vic Sower for his help with some of the technical aspects of putting this book together. We also appreciate his creative ideas for activities for some of the centers. We extend our thanks to our student assistant, Mary Jane Guerrero, and to Kassandra Hughes in our Language, Literacy and Special Populations Department at Sam Houston State University for her assistance in decorating some of the boxes used in the pictures.

TABLE OF CONTENTS

Introduction

Too often, teachers fail to make use of one of the most powerful and motivating methods for teaching young children, the learning center. This book is a beginning point toward getting you to think in creative ways as you develop these centers and others. Once you actually observe your students working in learning centers that are specifically designed for the skills taught in your classroom, you will want to continue and even expand your use of learning centers.

All of the centers in this book are appropriate for children ages 4–7 years old, with modifications being made for a particular age. The skills for 4-year-olds will focus on those such as counting, sorting, and beginning reading skills. Older children will be expected to use more advanced skills such as measuring using rulers and scales, counting money and making change, and more difficult activities involving reading and writing in the centers.

Young children need to practice skills in many different settings and with many different materials in order to grasp and transfer concepts. Learning centers provide a very natural, fun way for them to do this through the use of dramatic play. With careful planning, teachers can differentiate learning activities in the centers for all of the levels of learning in their classrooms.

We have also included many unique ideas for you to use with your children, not the "same old" things that other teachers will be doing or have done before. By making experiences unique, you can encourage your students to become interested in many different areas of study: reading, writing, science, math, social studies, music, and art. Children will want to come to school each day, behavior problems will be diminished, and your students' enthusiasm will encourage you in your use of centers.

Chapter 1

Why Children Need Learning Centers

Jason, Cole, Bralyn, and Drew were playing in the block center when Jason exclaimed, "Let's build a cow!" Responding quickly, one of his friends said, "Won't we need some boxes to build a cow—and paint?" Drew solved the problem by suggesting that their teacher would be able to help them gather the materials they needed to build a cow—cardboard boxes, glue, paint, small pieces of felt, twine, and space in the classroom for construction to begin.

After a few days, the cow became reality. Their teacher, Ms. Robertson, provided time for the boys to share their construction with the other children in the class, suggesting that each one tell how he was involved in the project. "I added the tail," said Bralyn proudly, while lifting the twine for all to see. "We all painted," Jason commented. "I made the ears," Cole added.

Learning centers of the nature described here are the backbone of learning in early childhood classrooms. From the earliest history of early childhood education—from Froebel and Montessori, to Dewey and Piaget—and now in contemporary times, experts in the field have believed that learning in classroom centers is critical to children's development (Albrecht & Miller, 2004; Byrnes, 2001; Warner & Sower, 2005). Many early childhood classrooms already have established centers that stay in the room year-round like the home living center, the art center, the block center, and the book center. This book adds to those centers by discussing the use of more specialized learning centers. What follows is a discussion of some of the multiple reasons why children need both types of learning centers, including that:

- learning centers provide children with choices,
- learning centers help meet children's needs,
- learning centers help children build skills,
- learning centers are valuable to the learner who has special needs,
- most classrooms plan for traditional learning centers, and
- teachers can create learning centers easily.

LEARNING CENTERS PROVIDE CHILDREN WITH CHOICES

Whether children choose the home living center or the book corner, their opportunity to make a selection allows them to view themselves as people who are in charge of their lives. Preschoolers have so few opportunities to feel as if they are in control. Their families (and teachers too) make most of the decisions about what they will eat, the clothing they will wear, where they will go, what activities they will participate in, what television programs they watch, what time they go to bed, and the list goes on and on. Making choices at learning centers helps them feel powerful. Of course, they also learn about living with the selection they made, especially if adults guide them to stay with their choice for a while.

LEARNING CENTERS HELP MEET CHILDREN'S NEEDS

Classroom learning centers match children's developmental needs. Above all else, children need activity. They need to move, explore, and expend their energy. Being engaged in learning center activities allows them to learn about their world in a meaningful way, work with others, make decisions about their play, and totally enjoy the experience. Most of the time, children are participating at optimum levels of learning because they find pleasure in their actions. Not only do they interact with others, as in the cow example described above, but they also are challenged to new levels of understanding about their world because of their interactions with others.

CHILDREN LEARN THROUGH PLAY

Sometimes, parents and other adults question the use of play in preschool classrooms. In the current age of accountability, learning center activities look like wasted time. "What are children learning?" some people ask. "Is the money we're spending on their education just being wasted?" The answer is simple if you take a close look at the play going on in classroom learning centers. Children are learning! Here are some examples of children's learning in centers commonly found in primary classrooms:

- The child in the art center is acquiring valuable planning and organizational skills, plus using creative thinking in the process.
- Children in the block center learn information about the formation of structures, as well as math (e.g., sizes and shapes of blocks) and science skills (e.g., how to balance a stack of blocks and the weight of blocks).

- Children in the home living center are developing social skills (e.g., learning to get along with one another) and playing roles they will need for adult life.
- A child in the book corner finds enjoyment in a book, whether she can read it or not. Looking at pictures will suggest a storyline, but if she wants, she'll find someone who will share the text with her.
- Writing centers give children opportunities to explore what print can do.
- The grocery store center helps children participate in an event that their families may or may not allow them to do. They learn to categorize foods and nonfood items, how to make purchases, and the socialization necessary to be pretend consumers.

Lilian Katz and Sylvia Chard (2000) referred to children's play while doing projects cooperatively as the informal aspect of classroom curriculum. They recognized that formal instruction is necessary as children grow, but they believed that children's intellectual development and positive attitudes toward learning are linked integrally to their spontaneous play. Play benefits include children's application of skills and their motivation and interest in their self-selected activities.

Most early childhood professionals agree that play is critical to children's readiness for school and reading. In *Children's Play: The Roots of Reading* (Zigler, Singer, & Bishop-Josef, 2004), several experts agreed that play:

- develops thinking skills,
- supports children's understanding of symbols,
- encourages language development,
- serves as context for the development of literacy skills,
- motivates children to learn because of its relevance, and
- helps children make friends.

What is of utmost importance, though, is the role of play in helping children develop self-control. Vygotsky's study (as cited in Bodrova & Leong, 2007) of children indicated that self-regulation (their ability to plan and govern their own behavior) is related to their participation in play activities. Children who can self-regulate are capable of learning what they need to function effectively in classrooms (Bodrova & Leong, 2007). Self-regulation provides the framework for children's imagination and their ability to act out roles and behave within the restrictions of the role. In other words, a child who takes on the role of "dog" in a play setting will behave only as dogs behave and not in some other role.

LEARNING CENTERS HELP CHILDREN BUILD SKILLS

Children best remember the skills they learn when they are "up close and personal," so to speak. Adult learning is no different—we remember what we do. Try learning to play a musical instrument without being engaged. Have you ever tried to learn a foreign language without speaking it? Play allows children time to learn what they need to know about what goes on around them—socially, emotionally, cognitively, and creatively (Gestwicki, 1999).

Here are some of the specific skills children learn in the centers found in most early childhood classrooms (Warner & Sower, 2005):

Home Living Center
- Social skills and roles
- Practical living skills
- Language and vocabulary development
- Collaboration with others

Manipulatives Center
- Attributes of objects (e.g., size and shape)
- Mathematics skills (e.g., patterning, seriation, classification, matching, numbers, sequencing)

Writing Center
- Experimentation with pencil and paper
- Concepts of print
- Fine-motor skills
- Cutting with scissors
- Emerging writing

Art Center
- Fine-motor development
- Art elements (e.g., line, color, space)
- Use of art media
- Self-expression
- Creativity

Block Corner
- Mathematics skills (e.g., balance, height, length, proportion, organization, shapes, patterning)
- Construction skills

- Problem-solving skills
- Collaboration with others

Book Center
- Concepts of print
- Care of books
- Language and vocabulary development
- Story sequence, plot, and characters
- Foundations for reading

Music Center
- Appreciation of music
- Singing
- Musical concepts (e.g., pitch, tempo, melody, dynamics)
- Language and vocabulary development
- Aural discrimination

Outdoors Center
- Gross motor development
- Pleasure in nature
- Physical abilities and development
- Endurance
- Simple group games
- Physical knowledge

CENTERS ARE VALUABLE TO THE LEARNER WHO HAS SPECIAL NEEDS

Not only are classroom learning centers important to young children, but they also are particularly important to children with special needs. The child with a learning disability needs practice with the skills he is acquiring. Children with autism, for example, need opportunities to rehearse skills over and over. Many of the teaching strategies used with children who have special needs are repetitive, and teachers ask these children to practice again and again. Children who are gifted also need to have activities that are challenging and interesting. Learning centers allow children, whether they have special needs or not, to practice skills in nonthreatening, pleasurable ways on a level that is appropriate for them.

MOST CLASSROOMS PLAN FOR TRADITIONAL LEARNING CENTERS

Teachers in the early education field recognize that certain learning centers are traditional to the early childhood classroom such as the home living center, manipulatives center, blocks center, book corner, art center, and music center. Many teachers maintain a set of classroom dolls to aid students in their imaginative play. The playground usually becomes an outdoor center. Even when classrooms are small, at least three or four of these centers are present.

At the beginning of the year, teachers introduce classroom learning centers to their children and define some basic rules about how each is to be used. Generally, children are given choices of learning center activities and the numbers of children at each learning center are limited to avoid management issues. As the year progresses, new toys, equipment, and materials are added to learning centers to maintain children's interest in their play.

TEACHERS ADD OTHER LEARNING CENTERS

Teachers also rely on adding other learning centers throughout the year, which might accompany a special study the children are doing or focus on skills that children might need. For example, preparing a discovery center during the fall season so children can investigate nature's changes (e.g., colorful leaves, acorns or nuts found on the playground) sparks a renewed educational interest for some children. Learning centers, whether they are traditional or unique in design, help children develop cognitive concepts while experiencing a pleasurable outlet for their boundless energy.

Differentiating Instruction With Centers in the Inclusive Classroom is a book about other learning centers teachers might develop for their children throughout the school year. Putting props and materials into a box that can be stored easily helps teachers who have no room for numerous learning centers in their classrooms. Once teachers observe children working in the learning center boxes, they will see how efficiently they can observe and evaluate the skills most often introduced in primary classrooms.

SUMMARY

Classroom learning centers benefit children by giving them choices; meeting their social, emotional, physical, and intellectual needs; and building their cognitive skills. You will learn information about organizing classroom learning centers in Chapter 2.

Chapter 2 Organizing Your Learning Centers

Having enough classroom space can be a problem in many early childhood classrooms. The learning centers in this book are designed so that all of the materials will fit into a box. Often the box is actually part of the center itself. It may be an oven in one center, a bank vault in another center, or a counter/display case in a third center. Each box can be designed so that it fits in within the center. For the most part, cardboard boxes that once held copy paper can often be obtained at copy shops for free. These boxes work well for holding center materials. Once the children have begun to tire of the center, all of the materials can be stored back in the box and then placed in a storage area until the next time that you want to use it.

This chapter will walk you through the process of developing learning centers for your classroom. You will find information on the following:

- planning new learning centers,
- developing specific skills,
- involving children in planning the centers,
- creating a box for each center,
- assessing students,
- assembling the learning centers, and
- observing students at play.

PLANNING NEW LEARNING CENTERS

When developing new learning centers for the classroom, it can be extremely helpful for you to visit a store that mimics the type of center that is being planned. For example, when developing the hardware store center, visit a hardware store. Walk up and down the aisles, look at the merchandise, and make a list of items that you might want to include. After touring the store, ask to speak to the manager, and tell him or her that you are making a learning center for your classroom. Managers have been known to donate short lengths of PVC pipe, washers from opened containers, paint stirrers, damaged peg board, bags with the store name, and other items. You can also ask the manager to save empty nail boxes and other items that will add realism to the center. Don't be shy about asking for items in stores. When managers know that you are making a center for young children, they are usually very forthcoming. Good teachers constantly look and think about experiences they can bring into the classroom everywhere they go.

Be creative when you set up your learning centers, either the ones in this book or ones you have developed. You will find that our ideas can be springboards to ideas of your own. Start by researching a new topic by using an online encyclopedia. This will open your mind up to new vocabulary words for the children, experiments that you might be able to do, and materials that you could have in a center.

DEVELOPING SPECIFIC SKILLS

After you have a list of the items you intend to put in the center, begin thinking about how the children can use those materials and develop your list of skills and activities that can be taught with those materials. One of the first places you should look for skills for the appropriate grade level will be on your state education website or on the websites of national organizations. These websites will inform you as to the skills that children are expected to master in each grade level. Knowing the skills you need to teach will assist you in developing appropriate activities.

Any of these learning centers may be adapted for any grade level from prekindergarten through second grade. The level will be determined by the skills appropriate for the particular grade level chosen, and the activities will be developed accordingly. For example, in the department store center, children in prekindergarten could sort the necklaces by color, count the jewelry into groups, and write numbers for the price of the items. Second graders could use the same materials, but they would draw blueprints of their home showing placement of appliances, measure the necklaces using rulers, weigh them using postal scales, and write descriptive sales ads for department store items.

INVOLVING THE CHILDREN

Always involve the children in planning and developing a center. When they become enthusiastic about a center, you are more likely to get parent involvement in sending items that you need. To involve families, write a parent letter about the center (see Chapter 5), beginning with the list of materials that you need. Parents are very willing to donate materials and/or save items for you. They have even been known to offer materials that you might not have thought of using in your center, so be very open to their offers or ideas. One way to safeguard small items that the parents have loaned you would be to purchase a large shadow box that locks. Items placed in here would be safe from little hands. If you know someone who is handy with carpentry, he or she could build you a display case that could be placed on a table or desk. This could be used for many of the learning centers, and the children could even use it to display special items of their own.

Parents may also be willing to lend their expertise and assistance in the center's preparation. Again, using the hardware store example, one parent might have unused bins that he is willing to donate to the center for sorting screws and washers. Another parent might be willing to make a rack where screwdrivers can be hung in order from shortest to longest. Another parent might have some unused pegboard hooks. Notes home to parents will often result in donations such as these. The children's excitement as their parents help will have the students eagerly awaiting the opening of the center.

CUTTING THE BOX

Find a box and make the necessary modifications to it. If you use it as a counter, you might want to consider cutting out a display case on the long side of the box. This can either be a door that can be opened and closed and used for storage of items, or it can be an open area that you cut out and then tape a clear report cover or piece of Plexiglas over the opening. This then becomes the display window in your counter.

The following instructions will help you make the most common, basic cuts to your learning center boxes:

1. *Door.* A door can be cut into the long side of the box. Cut the door so that about 3 inches of box remain between the door and the edge of the box. The door can open down or to the left or right. See Figure 1.
2. *One open side.* Place the box on the table and remove the lid. On one of the long sides at both corners, you will need to cut down from the top edge to the bottom, freeing this side. Fold the long side out. See Figure 2.
3. *Three open sides.* Begin by making the one open side cut, cutting and folding down the long side of the box. Now cut along the bottom of each of the short sides, and fold the end pieces out in a 45-degree angle. This leaves only the remaining long side connected to the bottom of the box. See Figure 3.
4. *Open ends.* On the short sides, draw a line down from the middle of the top edge to the bottom. Cut down this line on both short sides. At the bottom of

the box on the short sides, cut the box from the first cut along the bottom to the corners, freeing the short sides. Fold these side pieces out.

ASSESSMENT USING THE LEARNING CENTERS

The two assessment scoring sheets in Appendices A and B can be reproduced and then completed by you for the assessment of the children. You will fill in the blank lines with the appropriate skills that are being reinforced or taught with the center. You can save time by filling out one copy of the class assessment sheet with all of the children's names and using this as a master. As new learning centers are introduced, you can copy the master and add the skills for the new center. Further information about using the assessment sheets can be found in Chapter 4.

ASSEMBLING THE LEARNING CENTER

Now that the materials have been collected, you are ready to begin assembling your center. Decide where to put the center, then arrange the box and all of the materials in an attractive manner. During center time, stay in the center and have small groups of children visit the center as you explain how to use it, what the different activities are, and what rules or limits go along with the center. Be sure to give each group some time to actually play in the center. Common limits might include telling the children that the materials need to stay in the center, reminding them about being careful with certain items that might break, or cautioning them about keeping up with small parts. Be specific when you go over the limits that you have set with each center. Telling a child to be careful that materials may break is not as effective as saying that the plastic containers will easily break if they are bent or have heavy items placed on top of them.

WATCHING CHILDREN USE THE LEARNING CENTER

Keep an eye on the center and restate limits as needed. Also, observe the children as they play in the center. Are they more interested in the buying and selling aspect of a store? If so, you could add play money, purses, and wallets to the center. Adding rulers, scales, and other items might also revive a center that the children are showing less interest in using. When the children are no longer playing in the center, you will know that it is time to put the center up. Pack all of the items back in the box and place it out of the way, until the children are ready to use it again.

Figue 1. Box cut 1: Door cut.

Figure 2. Box cut 2: One open side cut.

Figure 3. Box cut 3: Three open sides cut.

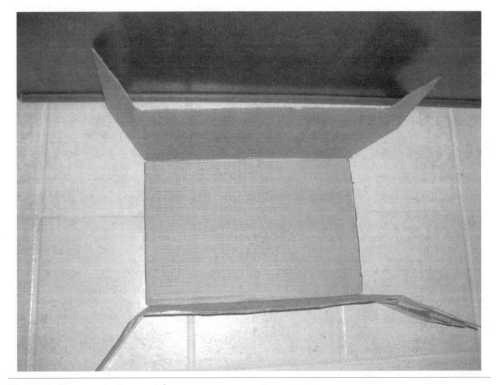

Figure 4. Box cut 4: Open ends cut.

HELPFUL HINTS

Paper boxes can generally be obtained for free at copy shops and office supply stores. Salt dough is easy to make (see Appendix C) and can be fashioned into all sorts of items for the learning centers. It is extremely durable and does not attract insects. It can be used to make everything from donuts to beads for stringing, and once it is baked until completely hard, it will last for many, many years. Secondhand stores, dollar stores, and yard sales are also good places to pick up items for learning centers at very reasonable prices.

You will find a glossary at the end of the book that will define some of the different skills and terms used in the book. Use this section of the book for ideas as to the types of skills that you can assess with each new center. Skills other than the ones listed for each center may be included.

SUMMARY

This chapter has explained the basics for putting together a learning center in your classroom, offered suggestions for obtaining material, outlined some of the basic ways to cut a box for use in your center, and described how you will know when it is time to remove the learning center from the classroom. The next chapter will provide suggestions for using this book.

Chapter 3 How to Use This Book

You have probably noticed as you looked through this book that descriptions exist for 31 centers. We know that this number of center studies is unrealistic for any one school year. We also know that most center studies will last more than a week; therefore, the centers presented in this book should be sufficient to span an entire calendar year. If your school year is shorter, you will need to choose centers that will match the interests and needs of your children.

You may have noticed, too, that we have organized centers by unifying themes (e.g., community centers, food centers, special interest centers, transportation centers, and just for fun centers). We have not recommended a sequence of themes, because we believe teachers should have choices as they organize for children in their classrooms. Teachers are more familiar with their respective communities, what areas of study will be more appropriate for their children, and the needs and interests of the children they teach. Our suggestion is that you select center studies based on your knowledge of your children, families, and communities.

We recommend that initially, as you begin organizing center boxes, you select five or six boxes to develop each year until you complete the entire book. If you work with a team of teachers, ask them to join you in preparing boxes. If each teacher completes several boxes, you can pass them around so all classrooms experience the various studies throughout the year, instead of relying on your own efforts to create each center described. As you teach, you can continue to organize boxes until you have completed your desired goal.

Each center discussion begins with a description of how the box may be used. This is followed by a list of contents for the box. You are not limited to using just these materials and should view this list as a starting point for the learning center, adding more materials as ideas present themselves. On the other hand, lack of any one material does not mean that this center cannot be set up. It may mean, however, that one skill being taught in this center may not be able to be taught. As there are many skills taught in each center, this would not seriously affect the value of the center.

HOW EACH LEARNING CENTER IS ARRANGED

As you work with children, you will note that some basic overview information about the box's contents is necessary when you introduce the center to your children. Each learning center in this book will provide you with the following information to guide your instruction:

- instructions for making the box,
- contents of the box,
- content information,
- vocabulary enrichment,
- dramatic play/cooperation,
- skills,
- other ideas,
- book connections, and
- items that families might donate or loan to the center.

The *content information* section provides knowledge to share with children, most often in a discussion. That information is the foundation for the dramatic play and skill development that will occur throughout the center's use.

As a corollary to content information, a *vocabulary enrichment* section is also included. Inherent in every study is children's language development, and teachers should use as many of the suggested vocabulary terms as possible as they develop discussions and model play experiences with their children. Our suggestions are not exhaustive, and teachers are encouraged to add other words that are pertinent for their children.

A section describing *dramatic play/cooperation* is designed to facilitate the intended use for each of these centers—children's play. Children learn how to interact with others, how to take on various roles, and new vocabulary words when they play with the contents of the center boxes. Teacher intervention should be minimal so children's creativity can emerge, but information can be introduced to youngsters when the teacher steps in to join the play experience.

Skills and *other ideas* are defined for each box study. Some activities are designed to extend children's knowledge about the topic of study, while others assist them in acquiring skills that are essential as a foundation for later learning. We have shared levels of activities from easy to more complex, so that the needs of all children can be met by the centers and all children can be successful. Skills listed may span the entire prekindergarten through second-grade levels. This list should be viewed as a starting point for the teacher. Teachers should consult their school, district, or state objectives when attempting to add other activities and skills. Identified skills should be shared with families through newsletters (more description about newsletters is shared in Chapter 5). This helps parents understand that their children are not "just playing" in school. Some suggested ideas for older groups of children might be appropriate for younger children who need challenges to keep them interested in the center's topic of study. Teachers will also find a glossary at the end of the book that will define different skills and terms used in the book.

The *book connections* section includes titles and authors of books that teachers might want to read and have available for the children while this center is being used. In addition, suggested *items that families might donate or loan to the center* will be included with each box description.

OTHER ITEMS YOU MIGHT NEED

Teachers will probably understand immediately that everything they might need for a specific topic of study cannot be included in one box. Some items (e.g., a cash register) will be used with several centers, so storing them in a box will not be possible. Other items (e.g., art materials) are disposable, and they will need to be replaced each year. Still other items are just too large to include in a paper box (e.g., children's wagons, child-sized wheelbarrow). Table 1 is a list of materials, toys, and equipment that should be available in the classroom throughout the year.

SUMMARY

This chapter has given you an idea of how to use this book and what types of information will be provided to you in each learning center. Chapter 4 will describe how to assess and document children's knowledge as they play.

Table 1
Items Needed for Classroom Learning Centers

Materials Needed	Toys Needed	Equipment Needed
Art supplies	Child's wagon	Stapler/staples
• Crayons	Child's wheelbarrow	Hole punch
• Markers	Wheeled toys	Open shelves
• Dry erase markers	Cash register	Child-sized tables and
• Children's scissors	Play money	chairs
• Paste or glue	Dress-up clothes	Tubs
• Construction paper	Purses and wallets	Pails
(variety of colors)	Jewelry accessories	Plastic baskets
• Butcher paper	Play telephones	Plastic divided trays
• Tissue paper		Rulers
• Gift wrap		Yardstick
• Manila paper		Scales (balance and
• Poster board (variety		postal scale models)
of colors)		Digital camera
• Ream(s) of paper		Classroom computer
• Masking tape		
• Colored masking tape		
• Duct tape		
• Yarn		
• Twine		
• Index cards		
• Sponges		
• Cardboard (including		
corrugated cardboard)		
Food items		
Cleaning supplies		

Chapter 4   Assessment of Children's Play

The current trend in education is to focus on documentation of children's learning. This age of accountability requires teachers to know how and why assessments of children's learning are critical in their classrooms, regardless of whether they teach in public or private settings. Agencies who provide funds for early childhood classrooms want to verify that the monies they are providing are being used beneficially to educate young children. Local, state, or national funding sources expect teachers and administrators to describe the learning that's going on in their classrooms to families, legislators, agencies, or other interested parties.

As a teacher, you need to know what children are learning for several important reasons:

- making sound curriculum decisions,
- preparing for conferences with parents or guardians,
- showing that you are doing a credible job in your position, and
- documenting your understanding of developmentally appropriate practice.

First, you need to know what children are learning in order to make sound curriculum decisions about what is to be taught (McAfee & Leong, 2002). If, in a preliminary screening of children's ability to count, you discover that Collin cannot count rationally beyond five objects, then you can organize instruction to assist him in learning how to count objects beyond five. Your screening process may suggest to you that Collin can count by memory to 20 or even 25, but counting objects is beyond his ability. If you also discover that Emily and Mindy are unable to count rationally, then you can plan for small-group instruction to work with these three individuals. In a nutshell, assessment informs curriculum (and, consequently, classroom instruction). More information about making curriculum decisions follows in this chapter.

A second reason for assessing children is in preparation for conferences with parents or guardians. Being able to tell parents that their children can identify eight colors, count to 10, name five basic shapes, write five alphabet letters (and tell parents which ones they are), and write their names when requested not only demonstrates that children are learning in the classroom, but having such knowledge of children's abilities shows your ability to teach what children are generally expected to know. As a byproduct of quality assessment, you can assist individual children in understanding how much they have learned by reminding them periodically of their progress in one-on-one conferences.

A third reason for assessing children is to show that you are doing a credible job in your position. You may want to share what you know about your students with your principal, especially if you want to recommend that individual children need special diagnosis and intervention. The evidence you provide will assist in making appropriate decisions for your students' education.

Lastly, having documentation of classroom teaching and learning is one of the essential components of developmentally appropriate practice. As a teacher of young children, you understand that assessment procedures must match the learner and provide instruction that matches the learner's specific needs. They must be " . . . culturally and linguistically responsive, tied to children's daily activities . . . and connected to specific, beneficial purposes" (National Association for the Education of Young Children & National Association of Early Childhood Specialists in State Departments of Education, 2003, pp. 2–3). Assessment is the process you use to determine what children know based on the learning opportunities they have in the classroom.

WHAT IS THE PROCESS OF ASSESSMENT?

Basically, there are two types of assessment: formal and informal. A formal assessment usually consists of a paper-and-pencil test, often standardized by national norms. In preschools and primary grades, however, most assessments are informal in nature, and you collect information about your children in casual ways. You use observation as a mainstay for collecting data, and you keep record of what your children have learned, looking at them both as groups and as individuals (Hyson, 2008). You use checklists and work samples children have produced to document your evaluation of their learning (often referred to as authentic assessment). Keeping a collection of information about children in portfolios provides an organizational strategy for showing others about children's progress. Some of the information you can learn about your children through observation includes whether children (Taylor, 2003):

- need further screening for vision or hearing;

- exhibit social-emotional behaviors that require intervention (e.g., being extremely shy, knowing how to join a play setting);
- need assistance with language development; and
- have fine-motor or gross-motor difficulties.

HOW IS LEARNING DOCUMENTED?

The true question becomes one of how you make the most of the opportunities to assess young children while they are engaged in classroom activity. Throughout *Differentiating Instruction With Centers in the Inclusive Classroom*, we have defined specific skills children will learn while playing in each of the described centers. If you value skill development, then you will plan activities that strengthen children's skills and allow time for their repetition.

If you also value the importance of learning center experiences, then you will use your observational skills to document the learning children are acquiring. For example, let's say that you want to tell families in your classroom that children are learning specific mathematics skills. By watching individual children, you can support your statement by collecting information with a prepared checklist in order to accurately describe the learning each child is doing. Here are some classroom examples:

- *Post office center*: You notice that children are writing numbers on envelopes to represent their own or others' addresses (recognition of numerals).
- *Paint and hardware store*: You observe children working together to count the numbers of nails in a jar (counting). When they group the nails together in twos to count them, you make a note so that you can inform families of the knowledge they are gaining (counting by twos).
- *Ice cream parlor*: The children start a display showing everyone's favorite ice cream flavor (graphing).
- *Office center*: The children use the typewriter or keyboards placed in the center, and you make a note that they are recognizing letters and numerals (letter and numeral recognition).
- *Camping center*: You encourage small groups of children to plan a 3-day menu for a camping trip and determine food items that will be needed to use the plan (organizing and writing).
- *Sports store*: You notice individual children looking at pictures of sports stars and identifying their uniform numbers (recognition of numerals).
- *Department store center*: You provide a nonstandard measure so children can measure a length of yarn 10 inches long for stringing beads (measurement).

Not only can you describe the learning individual children are doing in private conferences with families, but you can report your observations more generally in newsletters that you routinely send home. Informing families of the skills children are exposed to is another strategy for documenting teacher effectiveness.

HOW TO BECOME A BETTER OBSERVER

The specific tips for becoming a good observer of children's activities in centers include:

1. Develop a checklist of skills that you want to observe (independently or with other teachers). In this book, specific skills are suggested for classroom use with each of the described centers. Sample checklists and how skills are listed and documented for observation purposes are described. Note that blank assessment forms are located in Appendices A and B for classroom use. Copy the forms and write in the skills that you desire to document.

2. Determine whether you will be observing individual children or groups of children. Place the checklist on a clipboard and situate yourself as close to the center as possible without appearing too obtrusive. Children will ask what you are doing, of course, and you can tell them that you are gathering information about their learning to share with their families.

3. Spend approximately 20 minutes observing children and listening carefully to what they are saying. Lengthen the time you spend in observation as you deem necessary.

4. At the end of the day, look again at the data you have collected. Use this information to make lesson plans for individual children or small groups of children who need additional assistance with specific skills.

5. Make sure that you post a date on any data you have collected about children. Showing progress for each learner requires documentation of the work he has produced.

6. Formulate a plan for sharing information with children's families. Conferences are a good time to tell about children's progress, but you can use notes or letters home and phone calls as well.

If you are using a portfolio to collect checklists and children's work samples, consider using video clips of children or cassette recordings of their play if your school has the necessary equipment. These demonstrate specifically to parents or guardians that children are making progress socially, emotionally, and cognitively. With emerging expertise as an observer, you may be able to define children's specific approaches to learning (McAfee & Leong, 2002).

MAKING CURRICULUM DECISIONS

The strength of assessment is that the process coordinates well with classroom instruction (McAfee & Leong, 2002). If children are lacking skills and abilities they need for success, then assessment reveals their needs. Looking at children while they are learning gives teachers insight about the environment, schedule, materials, and equipment, as well as classroom procedures, which affect how children acquire knowledge. Caring teachers adjust their instruction and modify the classroom environment accordingly.

For example, as children play in the office center, you might recognize that youngsters need additional materials so they can continue to pretend to be office assistants. Think about sending out a request to families for discarded keyboards to place in the center. Children need challenges as their learning develops and adding more keyboards accomplishes the need for children to move beyond the original intent of the center.

The statement that "assessment informs curriculum and instruction" tells us that what we know about children and how they learn (assessment) provides insight about how to teach them (instruction). Here are concrete examples of this decision-making process:

- Mrs. Berry noticed that several of her children playing in the bookstore center were grouping the books together by the first letter of the book title. She said to them, "I notice that you are alphabetizing our books. Here are dividers to help you separate the books on the shelves alphabetically."
- Ms. Cotton realized that within a few minutes of introducing the department store center to her children that the entrance was not wide enough for Marcy to enter. Marcy uses a wheelchair while she is in school because of a birth defect that caused partial paralysis. Ms. Cotton adjusted to meet Marcy's needs by rearranging a few pieces of furniture so Marcy could have wheelchair access.
- Ms. Sharon became aware that Delton, one of her more shy children, was sitting in the book corner looking at a book about dinosaurs and calling them by their scientific names. "Wow, Delton," she commented, "I didn't know you knew so much about dinosaurs. If you're willing, I would love for you to share your knowledge with other children in the class when we have group time. What do you think about that?"
- Mr. Beard began displaying simple instructional charts for his children who were beginning to understand that print has meaning. He continued to give verbal instructions for special activities, but he wanted to challenge the children who were gaining more knowledge about print. The first chart he put up was a written copy of the instructions for a recipe for making ants on a log.

- When Ms. Caitlin recognized that the farm and farm supply center had lost its appeal to the children in her class, she made a decision to open the camping center.
- Mr. Franks recognized that some of his children were marking tallies to keep a record of the numbers of crayons there were in the crayon basket. He entered their play and said, "Hey, guys, let me show you a new way to mark tallies. You can count by fives if you mark four lines and put a diagonal line across the first four like this." (He demonstrated the procedure.) "Then all you have to do is count 5, 10, 15, 20, and so on. If you need more help with the tally process, let me know."

As you can see from these few examples, assessment and the decision-making process are ongoing events that complete the learning and teaching cycle that good teachers plan in their classrooms. Intentional procedures for assessment warrant intentional practices for children to maximize what they learn every day. More information about how to use assessment information appears later in this chapter.

EXTENDING LEARNING

Because of the ongoing observations of the children, teachers will be quick to notice in which areas it might be possible to take the center in another direction or where higher level skills seem to be appropriate for some of the children. Often just the addition of new materials to the center is all that is needed. When Mr. Ruiz noticed that the children in the bakery center were showing interest in labeling the bakery items, he added the appropriate paper and markers and suggested to the children that they might want to add signs to the bakery. They could label the items and include prices for the various baked goods. He later noticed that the children were using the play money more. Mr. Ruiz again extended the learning of the children by giving the children a sorting tray for the coins and dollars. Small change purses and wallets and a cash register were also added as children become more interested in the money side of operating a bakery. Some children, depending upon their prior experiences, might even be ready to learn the names and amounts of the various coins.

HOW TO USE ASSESSMENT INFORMATION

Keeping track of your assessments of the children by using forms makes it easy for you to plan your instruction. Each type of assessment has particular advantages. When you use the individual child assessment sheet (Appendix B), you are gathering information on a particular child. This information can be used in parent conferences. Because there is room for comments, you can make note of such behaviors as "made no attempt." This would indicate that the child didn't or wouldn't attempt the skill. This gives you more information than just having a blank box. Why didn't the child attempt this skill? What and how can you assess this skill in another way? The class assessment sheet, on the other hand, allows you to see at a glance which children may need help with specific skills. These children can then be pulled into small groups for further instruction.

USING THE CLASS ASSESSMENT SHEET

Using the bakery class assessment sheet in Figure 5, you can see, as one example, that Andy didn't master counting to 12, the three sounds, and the color words. Looking at the chart in more detail, you see that you can pull Ethan and Hannah for further work on counting to 6. You have another group who needs help counting to 12 that consists of Abby and Lupe. Hannah and Ethan will join them when they have mastered counting to 6. Another small group will have Andy, Charlie, Drew, and Lupe work on the sounds of /f/, /s/, and /n/. The last small group will master the color words yellow, red, and green. Andy, Briana, Ethan, Hannah, and Joanna will be in this group. And, because only three of the children mastered graphing, you will need to provide many more experiences for all of the children in this area. Many activities can be done as whole class, and you can use the children who understand graphing to try to explain it to those who don't in another way.

With each small group you will plan concrete, interesting activities that will facilitate mastery of the skills. Counting to 6 can occur as Hannah and Ethan make bags of six cookies for the pretend picnic or count six donut holes for a customer. The group working on the sounds /f/, /s/, and /n/ can participate as you have the children find an item among many that begins with the same sound as napkin, fork, and sack. Once the children are being successful with this game, it can be expanded to find something in the room that begins with these sounds. The color words can be worked on using paint, playdough, markers, songs, and games.

Because Phillip was the only child who had trouble with dramatic play, you can work with him at the center. Phillip, who is an only child, is very reticent about joining other children in dramatic play. He often plays by himself. When you engage Phillip in play in the center, it won't be long before other children will join him. Phillip will be more comfortable because he is used to interacting with adults. Other children will want to play with you, the teacher. Because of this, you have now facilitated play between the other children and Phillip.

Child's Name	Skills	Dramatic Play	1 to 1 Correspondence	Matching	Counts to 6	Counts to 12	Extends Patterns	Makes New Pattern	Sorts	Sounds f, s, n	Words yellow, red, green	Graphing
Andy		√	√	√	√		√	√	√			
Briana		√	√	√	√		√	√	√	√		
Charlie		√	√	√	√	√	√	√	√		√	√
Drew		√	√	√	√	√	√	√	√		√	
Ethan		√	√	√			√	√	√	√		
Hannah		√	√	√			√	√	√	√		
Isabel		√	√	√	√	√	√	√	√	√	√	
Jessica		√	√	√	√	√	√	√	√	√	√	
Joanna		√	√	√	√	√	√	√	√	√		√
Kenisha		√	√	√	√	√	√	√	√	√	√	
Lupe		√	√	√	√		√	√	√		√	
Manuel		√	√	√	√	√	√	√	√	√	√	
Oneita		√	√	√	√	√	√	√	√	√	√	
Phillip			√	√	√	√	√	√	√	√	√	
Rameisha		√	√	√	√	√	√	√	√	√	√	√

Figure 5. Completed bakery assessment sheet.

USING THE INDIVIDUAL ASSESSMENT SHEET

Because you also used the individual child assessment sheet (see Figure 6) as you first observed Ethan, you had room for comments and recorded that he wasn't interested in these activities and didn't attempt them. This is valuable information. Is the problem that he can't do these, or that he doesn't want to do them? You know that Ethan is very interested in Spiderman. Using this knowledge and some zoo animals that you also knows he likes, you can attempt to find out how far he can count. Pulling Ethan aside, display the animals, cages (made from berry containers), and a Spiderman action figure. Tell Ethan how the animals at the zoo all got out one day. The police called Spiderman to come help get them back into the cages. Then tell Ethan how many animals need to go into each cage, starting with a low number so he can be successful. You may discover that Ethan can count to 12 when he wants to do so. Because of the comments section on the individual assessment sheet where you had noted that no attempt was made, you realized that further assessment was needed. Had Ethan been unable to count to 6, then he would have needed to be in the small group for that skill. With further assessment showing that he could count to 12 when he chooses to do so, his participation in the small group was not needed. With fewer children in the group, each child receives more time from you. The use of these forms will provide you with a documented way to make decisions about individual children, about the curriculum, and about activities that need to be planned.

SUMMARY

Assessing and documenting children's learning requires your understanding of the assessment process and your abilities to accurately observe your children's learning. As a consequence, you can make important curriculum decisions about what children need to learn and how to extend their learning. The use of classroom and individual assessment sheets for all children gives you information for organizing individual, small-group, and large-group instruction and tracking the progress of individual children and the class as a whole. With this information, you are now prepared to talk to parents in a meaningful way. In the next chapter, you will find several ways to communicate with families.

Name: **Ethan** _____ School Year: **2009**

Skills	Date Tested/Comments:		
	3/1	3/8	3/12
Dramatic Play	Engages eagerly	✓	✓
1 to 1 Correspondence	Not observed	✓	✓
Matching	✓	✓	✓
Counts to 6	No attempt	No attempt	No attempt
Counts to 12	No attempt	No attempt	No attempt
Extends Patterns	✓	Completed AB patterns	Completed AB patterns
Makes New Patterns	✓	✓	✓
Sorts Into Groups	✓	✓	✓
Initial Consonant Sounds (f, s, n)	✓	✓	✓
Color Words (yellow, red, green)	No attempt	Confused red and green	Confused red and green
Interprets Graphs	Can't interpret graphs	Can't interpret graphs	Can't interpret graphs

Figure 6. Ethan's assessment sheet.

Communicating With Families

Chapter 5

Communicating with families about the progress of their children is an important responsibility of any teacher. You can enhance classroom instruction by:

- sending home regular newsletters,
- sharing your assessment documentation, and
- recommending opportunities that extend learning at home.

NEWSLETTERS

By sending home letters to families as each new learning center is introduced, you invite parents and guardians to be partners in their child's learning. Families can participate by saving and sending materials to school, donating materials, or loaning materials to the teacher for a specific center (always have families put their names on items they have loaned). Because they have been informed of the new learning center, parents are able to talk to their children about what is going on at school. By listing the skills that will be reinforced in specific learning centers, families are able to see that the children are not "just playing." Families are also able to gain an appreciation and understanding that their children can learn very specific academic skills through play. A sample letter is shown in Figure 7.

SHARING ASSESSMENT DOCUMENTATION

Parents and guardians have the right to know how and what their children are learning. An assessment sheet communicates with families, allows families to see their children's strengths and weaknesses at a glance, and provides insight into the

Dear Parents,

Our class is very excited about the new center we are planning: The Class Bakery. Below you will find a list of the needs we have for this center. Please send any of the items on the list to school with your child. We would like to open this center next week.

Items that we need for this center:
- Quart-size plastic containers (such as the ones that strawberries come in)
- Pint-size plastic containers (such as the ones that blueberries or blackberries come in)
- Plastic forks and spoons
- Napkins
- Old, used spatulas, wooden spoons, measuring spoons, and plastic or measuring cups

Skills that will be reinforced in this center are:
- *Dramatic play*: a fun and natural way to enhance a child's language and vocabulary development
- *1-to-1 correspondence*: a vital skill for children to possess before they can become readers
- *Matching*: another vital step in the reading, math, and science process
- *Counting to 12*: this is the actual counting of objects
- *Patterns*: being able to extend patterns and make new patterns is a skill that the children will need in order to be successful in all areas of math and science
- *Sorting*: being able to classify helps children build knowledge of how the world works and store that knowledge so it can be easily recalled
- *Initial consonant sounds*: these are essential for beginning phonics and reading
- *Color words*: being successful in early areas in reading help build a child's confidence in reading. Using concrete materials helps a child make connections to written words.

As you can see from the skills listed above, this center will help your child in many areas. Because the activities are fun, your child will be practicing these skills in a meaningful way.

As always, I much appreciate your help and assistance.

Sincerely,

Figure 7. Sample parent letter.

skills that their children have and have not mastered. Because parent and guardians are kept informed on a regular basis of both the strengths and weaknesses of their children (as opposed to just hearing about when their children need help), they will be more open to you in assisting their children when they need further instruction.

Assessment sheets also allow you to be able to suggest some ways that families can assist their children in mastering a specific skill. For example, when a child is weak in the area of patterning, the teacher can anticipate that the parents will ask for suggestions about ways to help the child. From talking with the child, the teacher knows that the child likes to color and has crayons at home. The teacher can suggest to the parent that he or she can begin a simple pattern with the child of alternating colored circles where the child has to extend the pattern. The parent can call it, "Guess My Color." Children often respond in a positive way when presented with any type of practice that is a game. If the child loves the outdoors, the parents can use acorns and leaves to create patterns that the child can extend. When the child understands a simple, alternating pattern, then the parent can make more complex ones. The teacher must be careful when speaking with parents not to use educational jargon or words that they might not understand. Often parents will not ask for clarification because they feel embarrassed to show that they don't know. So instead of telling the parent to make more complex patterns, the teacher might suggest different types of patterns: two acorns followed by one leaf; or one leaf, one acorn, one pinecone.

If the teacher writes down her suggestions for parents and then keeps these in a file, she will soon have a set of instructions for parents that can be used with other parents and from year to year. If several copies of these are kept readily available, then it becomes an easy matter to pull one out and give it to a parent as the teacher is talking to the parent about a specific student's needs. It is of the utmost importance for you to realize that you have the responsibility to communicate with parents and guardians and make them a partner in their children's educations.

IDEAS FOR FAMILY EXTENSIONS OF CENTERS

Families of young children are interested in their youngsters' school experiences. Consequently, when you make recommendations to enhance the learning that children are acquiring at school, you are strengthening the home-school connection. The suggestions described here demonstrate activities that should be easily organized and implemented by most families for some of the centers in this book. You can talk to parents or guardians informally about using extension activities as they pick up their children each day, or you can inform families in weekly or monthly newsletters.

When you talk to families about classroom learning experiences, encourage them to ask their children what they know about the topics they are studying. As they develop extensions in their homes, request that they give children opportunities to tell what they know. Family members can also ask children what they like best (or least) about the specific study theme. Also consider the cost of the suggested home extension. Most of the recommendations shared here will incur some financial commitment on the part of the family. You may choose not to make any recommendation to families if you know that they will be unable to afford the activity.

Community Theme Centers

- *Animal Hospital Center*: If you have a family pet (or using stuffed animals), talk to your child about illness and injuries that a pet might have, discussing the importance of the veterinarian's job.
- *Bookstore Center*: Take a trip to a neighborhood bookstore.

Specialty Store Theme Centers

- *Card and Party Shop Center*: Shop at a card and party shop for a birthday card for a friend or relative. Show children the variety of products this shop offers its customers.
- *Bed and Bath Shop Center*: Visit a bed and bath shop with your child, or show your child the bed and bath section of a department store.
- *Hair Salon Center*: Take your child along when one of your family members goes to a hair salon or barbershop.
- *Paint and Hardware Store Center*: Buy a tool or another item you need for your home at a neighborhood hardware store. Point out the store's various departments.

Food Theme Centers

- *Bakery Center*: Make a special trip with the entire family on Saturday morning to have breakfast at a neighborhood bakery. Some bakeries have their prep stations where children can see bakers at work.
- *Ice Cream Parlor Center*: Buy an ice cream treat for your child at this specialty store. Discuss how they keep the ice cream cold.
- *Pizza Parlor Center*: Have a family outing to a pizza establishment instead of ordering pizza. In some restaurants, children can watch the pizza being made.
- *Fast Food Drive Through Center*: Drive through a neighborhood fast food eatery to purchase food for your child. Explain how you order to your child.

Transportation Theme Center

- *Race Track Center*: Planning a trip to a car race is not always practical, because children tire easily. Watching a few minutes of a race on television is an option, or if your family watches movies, rent Pixar's *Cars*, a movie recommended for children age 5 and older.
- *Car Care Center*: When you take your car for an oil change or to have your tires rotated, give your child a chance to see the car care center.
- *Airport Center*: Visit a nearby airport, but plan on a short trip to prevent children from becoming overly tired.

Special Interest Centers

- *American Indian Center*: Find a book about the American Indian culture in your local library to check out and read to your children.
- *Farm and Farm Supply Center*: Visit a farm supply store during the spring to purchase tomato plants or seeds for a backyard garden. At any time during the year, you can visit a local farm.
- *Archaeology and Paleontology Center*: Take your children to a museum that displays fossils and skeletal remains of animals.

For Fun Centers

- *Camping Center*: Organize a family camping trip. Consider camping in the backyard if a trip out of town is not possible. Or, have a picnic in a city park or even in your backyard.
- *Amusement Park Center*: A trip to an amusement park is fun for the whole family if one is available. Amusement rides are more affordable when your community has a local fair.
- *Rodeo Center*: A rodeo is not always available to all families, but county fairs often have petting zoos for children to attend.

SUMMARY

Involving families in children's learning strengthens the critical home-school relationship and increases children's continued intellectual growth. Working with all children to help them grow intellectually implies that teachers must also plan modifications and accommodations for children with special needs. How to plan for children with special needs follows in the next chapter.

Modifying Classroom Centers for Children With Special Needs

Chapter 6

This chapter will discuss the use of learning centers with children who have special needs, both those who are gifted and talented and those with disabilities. In both situations, you should be prepared to adapt your learning centers to meet your students' needs.

CHILDREN WHO ARE GIFTED AND TALENTED

Children who are gifted and talented are underidentified and underserved in most classrooms. As a result, the needs of these children often go unmet. By using learning centers in the classroom, you can help meet the needs of these children, whether or not they have been formally identified. Because centers can be set up with many activities on many different levels, children are free to choose activities that are on a more challenging level, should they so desire.

Because so many children who are gifted and talented go unidentified, it is helpful for you to understand how these children are identified. The definition used by many school districts in defining children as gifted or talented is the federal definition from the Elementary and Secondary Education Act (1988):

> The term "gifted and talented," when used with respect to students, children, or youth, means students, children, or youth who give evidence of high achievement capability in areas such as intellectual, creative, artistic, or leadership capacity, or in specific academic fields, and who need services and activities not ordinarily provided by the school in order to fully develop those capabilities.

Schools use a variety of ways to identify these children. They may use test scores, recommendations from parents and/or teachers, and behavioral checklists. Parents may ask you how they can know if their children are gifted, especially when their children are young. You can share the following list of characteristics that might indicate that a preschool-age child is gifted (American Association for Gifted Children, 1999):

- Talks and reads early and has a large vocabulary.
- Demonstrates advanced language proficiency.
- Enjoys self-expression, especially in discussion.
- Has a unique learning style.
- Has a greater than average attention span.
- Asks many questions.
- Exhibits advanced observational skills and retains information about what is observed or read.
- Is challenged by problems, and chooses sophisticated activities, such as chess or collecting, as early as age 5.
- Shows interest in many kinds of books, atlases, and encyclopedias.
- Is interested in calendars, clocks, and puzzles.
- Is proficient in drawing, music, or other arts.
- Is driven to explore things, is curious, asks "why."
- Enjoys learning.
- Has wide-ranging, consuming interests.
- Interacts with adults more effectively than with children. (para. 1–3)

The United States Department of Education awards grants for programs directed toward gifted education through the Jacob K. Javits Gifted and Talented Students Education Act. The grants are based on scientific research, demonstration of projects, and innovative strategies (National Association for Gifted Children, 2010). One project that was funded from 2004 through 2009, Project Bright Idea 2: Interest Development Early Abilities, promoted the use of centers that addressed learning styles and multiple intelligences and provided task rotations in targeted public schools in North Carolina (American Association for Gifted Children, 2010).

Howard Gardner (2003) identified eight different intelligences that include abilities beyond what is easily measured by the typical IQ tests. His intelligences include: verbal/linguistic, logical/mathematical, visual/spatial, bodily/kinesthetic, naturalistic, musical, interpersonal, and intrapersonal. Verbal/linguistic and logical/mathematical intelligences are typically measured by IQ tests. Looking at children from this perspective helps parents and teachers recognize talents that are not measured by the typical school curriculum and create learning opportunities. For instance, a child who shows strength in the naturalistic area is very interested in the natural world. Reading and math activities become more interesting for the child as the teacher uses insects for counting or books about animals for reading.

Centers provide a perfect way to introduce interesting activities that will allow a child to practice, reinforce, or learn new information based on the child's natural interest or learning strength. Centers with books, reading, and opportunities to participate in dramatic play reinforce the child who is verbal/linguistic. Games, money, patterns, and numbers will appeal to students who are logical/mathematical. Visual/spatial learners will enjoy using design, artwork, and construction-type activities. Bodily/kinesthetic children will want to have activities that involve movement like dancing, dramatic play, and gross- and fine-motor activities. The addition of plants, animals, rocks, and fossils will help involve the child who has a naturalistic interest. Activities involving singing, humming, playing musical instruments, and listening to music and sound can be used to teach counting, letter sounds, math facts, or other information to the child with musical intelligence. Playing and interacting with other students make centers the perfect fit for the interpersonal child, while playing and interacting with the materials individually fits the intrapersonal child's needs. When you are aware of the strengths of the children in your class, you can add materials and activities to your centers that will enhance the learning of all of the children in your class.

How to Modify Centers for Gifted Children

It is unfortunate that some teachers think that making modifications for gifted children involve giving them harder worksheets or those from the next grade level. Instead, you need to incorporate higher level thinking skills, such as analyzing, synthesizing, classifying, inferring, and summarizing, in their daily activities. By analyzing objects and information, children would separate things into parts as they determine the nature of the whole. In synthesizing, children can reason from the general to a particular item or event. By first classifying items by organizing them into categories, students can then describe how they are organized. Using inferring, children can make conclusions based on evidence. In being able to summarize, students can present projects and results in a condensed form (Warner & Sower, 2005).

Keeping these skills in mind, as well as the theory of multiple intelligences, we've provided some specific ways to make modifications to the archeology/paleontology center activities as just one example of how to meet the needs of the gifted children in your class. The dramatic play/cooperation section of each center already meets the needs of children who are verbal/linguistic, bodily/kinesthetic, and interpersonal learners.

Specific Skills That Can Be Added to the Center For Higher Level Thinking

- Have the children sort the fossils into groups and then explain to the other children how they have been sorted (classifying).
- Add plastic jaws (or pictures) of carnivore and herbivore dinosaurs and have the children determine what the dinosaurs ate (synthesizing).
- Make a "midden heap" (the garbage dump) from an ancient village that has various seedpods, small bones from chickens, seeds, and nutshells and have the children determine the diet of the people (analyzing).
- Add various potshards (by breaking different shape ceramic jars, including only a few from each type of jar) to the midden heap and have the children decide what the shape of the jars might have been and what they might have been used for (inferring). Take pictures of the jars before you break them so that they can see how accurate their predictions were.
- Have the children make a presentation to another class about a "dig" in the midden heap from an "ancient" village (summarizing).

Activities in the Center That Already Address Multiple Intelligences

- *Sketching* (visual/spatial, bodily/kinesthetic, naturalistic, intrapersonal): With older children, when they uncover an artifact in the box lid, they can sketch it on graph paper.
- *Working with grids* (visual/spatial, bodily/kinesthetic, logical/mathematical, interpersonal): Before the children begin to dig in the box, they can lay out a grid using tape and string. The box would accommodate three strings being placed lengthwise on the lid of the box and four strings widthwise. The children can then use sticky notes to mark A, B, and C; and one, two, three, and four for the sections. When an artifact is found, they can record its location on the sketch (e.g., B2). Children also can hide artifacts in the grid and write the grid location for others to find.
- *Writing* (verbal/linguistic, intrapersonal): Have the children write information for a museum display about the artifacts that they recovered from their dig.
- *Weighing, measuring, and ordering* (logical/mathematical, bodily/kinesthetic, naturalistic, intrapersonal, visual/spatial): Have rulers, scales, and many different size fossils available. Children can weigh, measure, and order them in different ways.
- *Area* (visual/spatial, bodily/kinesthetic, logical/mathematical, intrapersonal, naturalistic): Have children trace fossils or bones on graph paper and

then figure out the area by counting the number of whole squares and estimating how many partial squares will make up how many whole squares.

- *Map skills* (visual/spatial, bodily/kinesthetic, logical/mathematical, intrapersonal, naturalistic): Children can locate different dinosaur finds in the United States on a map and then plan a "trip" to visit the different sites. They can write down the routes, figure the mileage, and research other sights to see on the trip.

- *Graphing* (visual/spatial, bodily/kinesthetic, logical/mathematical, intrapersonal, naturalistic): Have a box with a large number of fossils (with multiples of several types). Have the children create a graph to show the different types and amounts of fossils.

- *Reasoning* (visual/spatial, bodily/kinesthetic, logical/mathematical, intrapersonal, naturalistic, interpersonal, verbal/linguistic): Provide "bones" from several different dinosaurs along with the names of the dinosaurs, and have the children research the dinosaurs and decide which bone belongs to which dinosaur. You can also have cut tree rings and magnifiers for the children to count the rings for the age of the trees and to speculate why some rings are wider than others.

- *Exploring new technologies* (visual/spatial, bodily/kinesthetic, logical/mathematical, intrapersonal, naturalistic, interpersonal, verbal/linguistic): Have information and pictures of satellite photos, ground penetrating radar photos, carbon-14 dating information, and side-scan sonar for the children to study.

- *Other ideas* (includes all eight intelligences):
  o Visit a museum and notice how the artifacts are displayed and what information is provided.
  o Provide the children with meat trays and plaster of Paris. Take them outside and let them find a leaf to impress in the plaster.
  o Learn songs about dinosaurs. Write the words on a large chart and use that as part of reading instruction for the younger children. You can make up your own using a familiar tune.
  o Bring in books and magazines that show excavations with the grid laid out, and people using the brushes and other tools to uncover the artifacts. Look for websites that show current digs.
  o A sample dig could even be conducted on the school grounds. Depending upon the school's location, real fossils and/or Indian pottery shards might be found.

MODIFYING CLASSROOM LEARNING CENTERS FOR CHILDREN WITH DISABILITIES

Using learning centers as an essential part of the instructional day has many advantages for children with special needs. Use of learning centers affords children with special needs the opportunity to learn from their peers in a fun, nonthreatening manner. As children with special needs are playing, they are observing how their typical peers interact with each other. The children with special needs hear language used that may be at a higher level of development than their own. They also have the opportunity to practice their social skills.

Learning centers also provide a fun, appropriate way to continually practice skills that all young children need through a variety of different, but concrete experiences. For instance, children may practice counting by counting chocolate chips in the bakery center; again in the department store center as they count the number of necklaces that go in a box; and yet again in the bank center as they count coins into cash boxes. Although this may seem redundant, it is very important for young children, whether they have special needs or not, to have opportunities to practice the same skills in many different settings in order to transfer knowledge to new areas.

Research has shown that children with special needs greatly benefit from being included with other children. Using learning centers helps all of your students learn to appreciate the children in the class, even those who are different. When children with special needs are integrated within the classroom, their peers also gain by developing empathy for others who may have physical and/or mental challenges, helping others who may not be able to do things for themselves, and becoming more comfortable around people who are different from themselves.

English Language Learners (ELLs)

Incorporating learning centers into the instructional day is a perfect way to give the child who is an ELL an authentic way to develop new vocabulary by attaching meaning to new words. The National Center for Research on Cultural Diversity and Second Language Learning's Principle 7 clearly stated that "Language flourishes best in a language rich environment" (McLaughlin, 1995, p. 6). Teachers need to allow children to talk in order to experiment with language and become more proficient in its use. Teachers should find ways to increase social interactions and provide many opportunities for children to use language (McLaughlin, 1995). This need is easily met by using learning centers in the classroom.

By adding written words in the child's first language, you can assist the child in learning to read those words, and you have provided the opportunity for the other children to pick up words in another language. The child now has the opportunity to instruct the other children in his native language, while learning English at the same time. When children learn words from another language, they become very proud of their knowledge and like to use those words whenever possible.

Using learning centers and activities also allow children with limited English to demonstrate what they know in another, more concrete way. For example, a child may not be able to tell you that there are 15 cookies in the container, but he may demonstrate the concept of 15 because he sees the numeral 15 and can rationally count 15 objects. The National Association for the Education of Young Children (2009) took the position that teachers of culturally and linguistically different children need to "provide children with many ways of showing what they know and can do" (p. 2) and strive to find nonverbal ways for children to demonstrate their knowledge and skills. By using learning centers, you can observe a child and develop a better understanding of her actual abilities.

Speech and Language Delay

Children with speech and/or language delays will also benefit from being provided time to talk to and listen to other children in the classroom. According to the National Dissemination Center for Children with Disabilities (NICHCY, 2009d), "... a child's communication is considered delayed when the child is noticeably behind his or her peers in the acquisition of speech and/or language skills" (Fact Sheet #11). Playing with children who have more advanced language skills, in learning centers and elsewhere, provides these children with the language role models that they need.

You can help by structuring the classroom so that the child with the delay has the opportunity to spend quality time with children who have good language skills. Using learning centers allows an easy way for you to arrange this. You should consider playing in the center with the children. Your presence can encourage the other children to include the child with the delay in their scenarios, and you can ask questions that will add a new dimension to the play for all of the children. It is a well-known fact that where the teacher is, is where children want to be.

Attention Deficit/Hyperactivity Disorder (ADHD)

"As many as 5 out of every 100 children in school may have ADHD" (NICHCY, 2009a, para. 7). Because of statistics like this, it is very likely that you will have one child with ADHD in the classroom in any given year. Children who have ADHD have trouble attending to directions and controlling their impulsivity. Because of this, you should talk to these children individually and explain what constitutes acceptable behavior in the center, how the materials may be used, how they are expected to care for the materials, and all of the different tasks that can be done in the center. Once this has been done, however, you then need to realize that these children will still need constant reminders.

One of the needs of children with ADHD is to move on a regular basis. In a regular education classroom that uses learning centers, children have this need met. Regardless of grade level, when you have learning centers for your students to use after completing their work, instead of more worksheets, the children will be happier and better behaved because centers allow children to move as they use and manipulate materials. They are learning through doing.

Some children in the classroom may have ADHD-Inattentive Type, which means the hyperactivity aspect is not as pronounced. Children who have this type of ADHD will need to be monitored when learning centers are introduced. They may not pay attention as directions are given. It may even be necessary to go over this information with the child individually. Requesting that the child repeat back to you what has been said is one way to check for attention.

Autism

Autism spectrum disorders (commonly called autism) continue to make headlines in the news as science attempts to identify their causes. Autism affects boys four times more often than girls, and its incidence has been reported to be as high as 1 child in 110 having some form of autism (Centers for Disease Control and Prevention, 2009). This neurological disorder is characterized by communication problems, problems relating to others, problems with changes in routines, repetitive body movements, and repetitive movements with toys or other items (NICHCY, 2009b).

Children with autism do not handle changes in the daily routine well. You should watch which learning centers this child plays in most often and leave these learning centers up. When a new center is added, you need to make a special effort to introduce the center to the child. When you have a child with autism in the classroom, you must be cautious about a total rearrangement of the classroom. This might cause the child a great deal of stress and could possibly result in acting out behavior.

Visual Impairments

The visual impairments category of disabilities includes people who have partial sight to those who are totally blind. One of the characteristics of children with visual impairments is a hesitancy to explore their environment. This hesitancy may continue until the teacher makes the learning environment motivating and rewarding or intervention begins (NICHCY, 2009e).

Learning centers can be both motivating and rewarding for children with little or no vision, but you must make the effort to work with the child in the center and help the child to be able to do the various activities. Obviously, there will be some activities, such as matching by color, that the child may not physically be able to do. That should not discourage the child from using the center. You should go through all of the activities that the child can do in a hands-on manner. For example, the child would be able to sort items by shape by feeling them. Words should be typed in Braille in addition to regular print for the child to read. If low vision is a problem, large magnifiers should be in the classroom for the child to use when necessary.

Developmental Delay

The federal government allows schools to use the term *developmental delay* with children between the ages of 3–9, if the children are experiencing a delay in physical, cognitive, communication, social or emotional, or adaptive development (NICHCY, 2009c). Children with developmental delay will seem much younger than other children in the class in one or more areas. The modifications you use will depend upon the area of the delay. For example, if a child has a delay in fine-motor skills, the child might not be able to write, draw, or manipulate some of the items in the center as well as the other children. With this in mind, you might provide larger beads to string in the patterning activity in the department store center. Larger sticky notes for writing would also need to be provided, because the child would not have the control necessary to write prices on the smaller ones.

Although all children can engage in dramatic play at their own level, the activities that you have planned for special skills may be a problem. For children with cognitive delays, you might need to plan for several less difficult activities that the child can successfully do. The rest of the class might be able to match colored items to the color words, but a child with a delay may need to match items to pictures or to colored bins.

Children with developmental delays may also have problems in adaptive behavior and may be functioning at a much younger age socially. They might exhibit behaviors more typical of children 2 or 3 years younger than their age-mates. With this in mind, your expectations for the child should be more on the child's developmental level than her chronological age.

Physical Disabilities

The types of modifications for children with physical disabilities will depend upon the area of their body affected. Children who use wheelchairs will need to have activities placed on a table that their wheelchair will fit under. This will make the materials accessible and less likely that materials will fall on the floor and be unreachable. Children who have problems with control of their hands and fingers will need modifications made to each individual activity. In some cases, it may be necessary to have a buddy assist them or to have a low-tech device added that will assist the child in doing the task independently. For example, if the child is playing in the Card and Party Shop and wants to be the cashier, by cutting a small piece of dowel rod and placing a good size piece of sticky tack material on its end, you have made a low-tech device that allows the child to pick up the dollar bills and coins and hand them to another child. In other cases, a modification as simple as having larger beads or other materials available might be sufficient.

Each activity should be evaluated to see if there is a way to modify the activity, provide a low-tech device, or make some type of change that will allow the child to do the activity independently. In the department store center, earrings are to be matched and placed into a small, sectioned box. For a child with limited control of fingers and hands, bigger individual boxes might be all that is needed to allow the child to do the activity independently. Talking with an occupational therapist and/ or physical therapist can be very beneficial. These therapists are trained in thinking of ways to make modifications so that people with physical disabilities can be as self-sufficient as possible. They are usually more than willing to assist you.

Hearing Impairments

Children with hearing impairments may become isolated from the other students, if the other children have trouble communicating with them. You need to help your students use the same techniques that you use when talking to children with hearing impairments. It is important that you face the child with a hearing problem when giving instructions. This allows the child to gain more information about what you are saying by providing the child a view of your mouth. Some children can read your lips. You should not exaggerate words, but talk in a regular manner. By facing the child, you can also determine how much he has understood by looking at the child's face for signs of understanding. In addition, you should also model each of the activities for the child and then check for understanding by having him show you how to do the activity. If the child can read, written directions should be placed in the center. The directions would include a list of the activities and how to do them. Providing directions would also encourage the other students to read, so it would have a double benefit for the class.

SUMMARY

This chapter has provided you with ideas for making modifications to your learning centers for children who are gifted and talented or those who have disabilities. Keeping in mind the theory of multiple intelligences and higher level thinking skills, you can develop many suitable activities for gifted and talented children that will be exciting and enriching. The use of learning centers with children with special needs is one important way that you can arrange the curriculum to meet the individual needs of these children, as well as the other children in the classroom. It is important for you to be able to meet the needs of all of your children. The next chapter is the beginning of the actual description of the specific learning centers. It is arranged to include the learning centers based on the areas of the community that will be most familiar to the children.

Chapter 7 Community Theme Centers

Children are genuinely interested in their environment and everything around them. They begin recognizing businesses and food franchises in their community as early as 2 years old, and their first attempts to read include naming the stores they visit. If a family member mentions going to the grocery store or to the area mall, then young children are almost always eager to go along.

The learning centers in this chapter capitalize on children's interest in their community. Studying the stores or governmental agencies that families use regularly provides knowledge children may not have about the function of each and how they operate. As teachers observe and interact with children as they play in the centers, they can refine the information students have about each business and clarify misconceptions as they emerge.

ANIMAL HOSPITAL CENTER

Young children will enjoy playing with an animal hospital center. It gives them the opportunity to practice being an animal doctor and eases the worry you might have if you had a doctor's office center. (One prekindergarten classroom in our school had a doctor's office in the room and the teacher had to deal with an unexpected incident. She turned around and saw a child had stripped out of all of his clothes and was ready to "be examined" by the "doctor!") The animal hospital still gives the children the opportunity to be a doctor and use the equipment, but the patients are stuffed animals.

The bottom of the box in this center will be the examining table in the clinic. Use the door cut (see Figure 1) to create a door in the long side of the box. Cut the door so that about 3 inches of box remain between the door and the edge of the box. Make the door open down. The area inside the box will be used for storage of gauze, stethoscope, and other instruments needed to work on the animals. With the box bottom facing up, find a plastic tub or bowl and cut the box so that the tub or bowl will fit into it. Put the tub or bowl into the hole, and you now have a tub for bathing the animals. Place this on a table and assemble empty shampoo bottles, combs, and brushes around the tub.

For pills for the animals, use dried beans and peas and place them in small medicine bottles. Liquid medication can be made with water. If parents don't send any empty bottles, check with your local pharmacy to see if they will give you a few bottles or even sell you a few. Use stick-on labels for labeling the bottles with the medicine and the dosage.

Contents

- a supply of stuffed dogs, cats, hamsters, parrots, gerbils, and rats of various sizes
- bandages
- medicine droppers
- dog and cat collars
- pretend hair clippers
- gauze
- empty pill bottles
- medicine syringes
- liquid medicine bottles
- tape measure
- yardstick
- stethoscope
- blood pressure cuff
- play thermometer

Content Information

- Veterinarians are doctors who have animals as their patients. Most of the vets that the children may be familiar with deal with small animals, but there are also farm vets and vets for wild animals.

- The animal hospital is like the hospital is for people. These hospitals have medicines available to give the animals and can even do surgery on animals.
- Animal hospitals may also need to bathe an animal and cut the animal's fur as part of the treatment for the animal.
- Veterinarians give animals immunizations to keep them from getting sick, just like children get shots to keep from getting sick.
- Veterinarians give animals physical examinations and may prescribe supplements (like vitamins) for animals.

Vocabulary Enrichment

- veterinarian
- physical examinations
- humane
- breeds
- clippers
- grooming
- brushes
- shears
- prescribe
- muzzles
- personalize

- kennel
- obedience training
- disinfectant
- dose
- carriers
- ticks
- fleas
- coat
- life stages
- supplements
- immunizations

Dramatic Play/Cooperation

- Ask the children about their pets. Let them tell about their experiences with their pets and experiences, if any, at an animal hospital.
- Show the children the different instruments for working on the animals and explain why a veterinarian would use the instruments on the animals. Just like these stuffed animals, pets can't talk and tell the veterinarian what the problem is. The doctor has to examine the pet and try to figure out what the problem is and how to treat it.
- Mention some of the things that veterinarians may do for pets: examine them to be sure they are healthy, wash them in order to see a wound, treat a wound, put in stitches, give medicines, wrap up sores and wounds, operate, and set broken bones.

ANIMAL HOSPITAL CENTER

ANIMAL HOSPITAL CENTER

Skills

Counting

- Using some of the empty pill bottles, write numerals on them for varying amounts and have the students fill the bottles with the pills. These can then be placed in the pharmacy area of the hospital. As children learn to count rationally higher and higher, the numerals on the bottles can become larger.

Matching

- Make x-rays for a set of animal pictures. The children will have to match the leg bones with the limbs of the animals.

Uppercase and lowercase letters

- With laminated uppercase and lowercase letters designed to look like pill bottles, have students separate the pill bottles into two baskets. One basket will contain uppercase letters and the other one will contain lowercase letters.
- Make laminated cutouts of cats and collars. Place uppercase letters on the cats and lowercase letters on the collars. The children have to place the lowercase letters on the collars with the correct cat and its uppercase letter.

Sorting

- Give the children white Styrofoam plates and have them draw dog bones on the plates. Let them cut out the bones to use them for treats in the hospital. The children can then sort them into three groups by size. The bones can be stored in butter tubs in the hospital.

Estimating volume

- Have medicine bottles filled with liquid medicine (water) near the sink or over a tub. Have students estimate how many doses (one dropper full) are in each bottle. Then, let them use the medicine dropper to check their estimate by pulling up doses, counting them, and emptying the dropper into a small glass.

Writing

- Tell students their dog or cat is missing, and they should make a poster that describes their animal. The poster should include a phone number for contact, the dog's breed, color, size, and "answers to . . ." information. Have students draw a picture of their pet (or use the digital camera and take a picture of one of the stuffed animals).
- Tell students they are selling an animal. They must write a for sale flyer that includes the animal's weight, height, color, breed, and other descriptive words.

Measuring

- Have students measure a stuffed animal's height with a measuring tape, record the measurement, and then check their heights using a yardstick.

- Add a simple balance scale and have the children weigh the animals and order them from lightest to heaviest.
- Add a scale that measures in ounces. Have the children weigh the animals and record their weights on each animal's chart.

Following directions

- Create different illnesses or injuries for the stuffed animals, then provide step-by-step directions on what the students must do to treat the animal. For example, Fluffy has a cut on her front right limb. Take the medicated pad and place it on the limb. Wrap it with gauze three times around. Give her three antibiotic pills and place her in a kennel.

Other Ideas

- Discuss all of the different types of jobs that dogs can have (e.g., dogs for people with disabilities, search and rescue dogs).
- Invite a dog trainer to come into the classroom to show how dogs are trained.
- Invite someone with a dog helper to come to your class and show how the dog helps him. Tell students ahead of time that the dog is working, and that there are certain rules that need to be followed when dogs are working. One dog that visited our class with a person in a wheelchair wore saddlebags. The dog's owner showed a few of the things the dog could do: go into a bank and give the bank teller a check to cash and a money bag to put the money in, turn lights off and on, watch the traffic and safely guide the wheelchair across the street, and pick up the TV remote when it fell on the floor.
- Show pictures of all of the types of jobs that are available for people who want to work with animals: vets, groomers, trainers, handlers, and pet store clerks.
- There are many accessories for animals from clothing to jewelry. Show some of these to your students. Let the children design and make dog collars or other pet items. The hospital could "sell" these items.
- Have the children research different breeds of dogs and post information about the different breeds on a large poster. You might have them look for unusual information to put on the poster—the largest dog, smallest dog, a dog that doesn't bark, and so on.
- Ask a veterinarian if you may have or borrow x-rays for different animals to show the children.
- Have a discussion on the needs of pets and the responsibilities of pet owners.
- Find out how high dogs can jump (the record is 5 feet 6 inches, but you might want to go with a smaller breed's ability). Ask the children if they think they can jump as high. Do not give them any idea about how high this

ANIMAL HOSPITAL CENTER

is at this point. After they say whether or not they think they can jump this high, take them outside and mark the height on the side of the school. Challenge the children to try and jump as high as a dog.

Book Connections

- Ahlberg, A., & Clark, E. C. (1999). *Mrs. Vole the vet*. New York, NY: Puffin.
- Ardalan, H. (2001). *Milton goes to the vet*. San Francisco, CA: Chronicle.
- Blevins, W. (2002). *The vet's visit (Clifford)*. New York, NY: Scholastic.
- Liebman, D. (2000). *I want to be a vet*. Buffalo, NY: Firefly.

Items That Families Might Donate or Loan to the Center

- old medicine bottles and containers (ask the parents to thoroughly wash them before sending them to school)
- stuffed animals
- small, clean animal carriers (to kennel the sick stuffed animals)
- empty treat boxes and empty dog or cat shampoo bottles

ANIMAL HOSPITAL CENTER

DEPARTMENT STORE CENTER

Planning the department store center requires teacher knowledge about the department stores that are located in their community. Most small towns will have family-owned stores or businesses, while larger cities will have numerous department stores located in area malls. Your understanding of the type of department store children often visit will help you prepare a center box that contains relevant items for children's play. Talking to families or even conducting an informal survey will assist in your decision-making process.

In addition, department stores often offer a large variety of products to customers. Including representations of this variety in one small storage box is almost impossible; therefore, items will need to be gathered from your own home or from families who are willing to loan them or make a donation to the classroom.

Once you have made a decision about the department store you will highlight during the study, you are ready to prepare your box. If you wish, you can paint the box to look like a specific department store, especially if you want it to represent a locally owned business. You can print out or cut out the name of the store from an advertising flyer. Glue the store's logo onto one side of the box and seal it with clear contact paper. The box will be used as a counter to hold the classroom's cash register and other items (e.g., receipt books, pencils, markers) that children will use as they pretend to be sales clerks.

Position the box near small tables, which should be used to display department store products. Hang a clothesline from which to hang clothes for purchase by children as they pretend to be customers. One of the tables can be used as a gift-wrapping station. Another can be used for matching socks and organizing them into pairs.

Contents

- customer sacks from stores you are studying
- teacher-made signs indicating various department store sections (e.g., children's clothes, women's apparel, men's clothing, shoes, cosmetics, catalog orders, customer service, gift wrapping)
- empty cosmetic containers and perfume bottles, cleaned thoroughly
- doll clothes (for your classroom doll collection)
- fabric swatches (for children to make clothes to sell for dolls)
- catalogues
- jewelry
- small standing mirror
- Styrofoam head to display hats (if available)
- gift wrap
- old pairs of socks
- photographs of area department stores and their respective department store sections (stored in large freezer bags)
- clothesline for hanging clothes
- clothes hangers

Content Information

- Show photographs of community department stores so that children can make a connection to local franchises their families may have frequented. Ask children why they visit department stores. Show products that are often purchased in department stores.
- You might introduce the term *storeowner* to children and talk to them about the role of the owner in making decisions about what is sold, store hours, and who is hired to work.

Vocabulary Enrichment

- clerk
- customer
- storeowner
- store departments (e.g., cosmetics, women's apparel, children's apparel, accessories, men's wear, housewares, appliances, gift wrapping)
- dressing rooms
- customer service
- advertising circular
- exit
- restrooms
- elevator
- escalator

Dramatic Play/Cooperation

- Once the department store center is available, provide opportunities for children to use it in their play. Allow them to make decisions about who will be the clerk and who will be the customers.
- You can work with your children to make decisions about the various departments that should be included in the classroom store. Display section signs and explain to children what they are and what products are included in each section.

Skills

Fine-motor development

- Demonstrate to children how to fold towels and washcloths you have brought from home. Display these folded items on one of the tables in the department store center. You can also demonstrate how to fold clothes to place on display tables.
- Children might need instructions about hanging clothes on the clothesline. Be prepared to give them this knowledge if they need it.
- Place gift wrap on one of the tables in the department store center and provide children with tape and scissors so they can experiment with wrapping packages. Observe them as they work and step in if they need assistance

or tips as gift wrappers. Purchasing stickers for the station will also allow children to be creative as they decorate the gift wrap and improve their fine-motor skills simultaneously. If you add stamps and stamp pads to the table, children can design their own gift wrap creations on plain white wrapping paper.

- Give the children various lengths of yarn for the stringing of beads. Lengths could be typical lengths for necklaces (e.g., 10, 12, or 18 inches).

Matching

- Place photographs of area department stores and their sections on a table so children can match each store with their store sections. Provide a self-checking guide on the back of the photographs (e.g., a colored dot on those that are matches).

Pairing

- Use donated socks for children to put into pairs to sell in their department store. Make this activity more challenging by having pairs of socks that are of various sizes.

Ordering

- Have students hang T-shirts that have sizes marked on them from smaller to larger sizes in order.
- Bracelets and necklaces can be placed on a display rack according to length. This makes a pleasing display and provides an opportunity for the children to order the different items.

Comparing

- Have T-shirts that are premarked small, medium, and large. Have students compare them to shirts that are marked with specific sizes (e.g., 6, 8, 10). Which size is closest to each? Which size should you buy if the size you wear doesn't match perfectly? Why?

Subtraction

- Ask students: What is the difference between two shirts of different prices? Is there a reason that you would buy the more expensive one?

Design

- Have children design a new item of clothing or a new design for a T-shirt.
- Students can design a poster for a sales ad.

Reading and critical thinking

- Have students visit an online department store, check out the prices for a clothing item, and compare it to a sales ad for a local store. Students should list the advantages and disadvantages of making a purchase in each place. (Be sure to have them figure out the shipping cost.)

DEPARTMENT STORE CENTER

Other Ideas

- Place a large piece of butcher paper on a bulletin board in your classroom and divide it into department store sections. Ask your children to make recommendations about the various sections to use. Provide catalogues and scissors so the children can cut out items to glue into each section.
- Put large pieces of paper and pencils and/or markers on one of the department store tables so children can make sales signs and advertising circulars to place in the center.
- Talk to children about the difference between *small appliances* and *large appliances*. Ask children to cut out examples of each to go onto two different posters to display in the classroom. (*Note*: If children have difficulty while using scissors, consider allowing them to do torn paper art.)
- Encourage children to use fabric swatches to make clothes for the classroom dolls. They can glue the seams or staple them (some children may be able to use large needles and thread or embroidery floss with help from the teacher).
- Second graders will find a challenge in learning about the histories of nationally known department stores.
- If you have access to a diamond and a cubic zirconium, let the children use the jeweler's loop to try and see the difference between the two.
- Look online for a picture to show the size of the Hope diamond. Print it and talk about the cost of very large diamonds.
- Look for ads for jewelry and have the children compare ads for similar pieces. Why might one piece of jewelry be cheaper than another? (Quality of the stone is the answer.)

Book Connections

- Day, A. (1989). *Carl goes shopping*. New York, NY: Farrar, Straus and Giroux.

Items That Families Might Donate or Loan to the Center

- adult and children's clothing for dress-up play (request that parents put name labels in garments if they want them returned)
- adult and children's shoes for dress-up play
- empty cosmetic containers
- advertising circulars
- gift wrap
- old pairs of socks
- fabric pieces for designing doll clothes

BOOKSTORE CENTER

Children are drawn to books. They like handling them, reading them, and pretending with them. This center will appeal to children because the books are for more than just reading. They are the focus of the center and are sorted, sold, arranged, catalogued, and counted.

The box for this center does not necessarily have to be decorated. The use of the box should facilitate children's understanding of bookstores and their value to consumers. In contemporary practice, bookstores often sell many items other than books (e.g., videos, CDs, art supplies, T-shirts and other apparel). Some bookstores have coffee shops that serve as lounges for their customers, and they sell sodas and specialty coffees to buyers who want to browse in their store. If you're familiar with the type of bookstore your children may frequent with their parents, then this information should guide you as you plan the bookstore center you will set up in your classroom.

Placing the bookstore center near open shelves or a bookcase will promote children's dramatic play. The box itself can serve as a shelf if your space is limited, but you will probably want to display many more books than a paper box can hold.

If you do choose to decorate the box, find suitable pictures of books, videos, or CDs from magazines or advertising flyers that can be cut out and glued onto the sides of the box. Consider, of course, the type of bookstore you want for children's play as you make picture selections. Placing clear contact paper over the finished product will help your box sustain the wear and tear children's play will incur.

You probably will store only a few items in the box from year to year. One suggestion is to include dividers with alphabet letters on them to encourage children to put books into alphabetical order during dramatic play. You might store a few adult books (hardcover and paperback varieties) that children would see in a real bookstore. If you want, you might take photographs of an area bookstore to post on a classroom bulletin board. Sample souvenirs representing the community you live in (e.g., key chains, bumper stickers, postcards) would demonstrate to children the idea that bookstores sell more than books.

If you do not have an alphabet chart in the classroom to use, you might purchase one to include in your box to assist children in alphabetizing books. A poster that highlights the pleasure of reading from a teacher supply store can add an artistic dimension to your bookstore study; the American Library Association offers artistic posters annually. You also might find favorite books written in another language so children can compare them.

When you choose to study the bookstore topic, find books from your classroom book corner or the school's library to put into the center. Or you can check out fresh choices from your local library to bring into the classroom for a while. Be conscious of the various genres you include in the center. Consider picture books, pop-up

BOOKSTORE CENTER

options, paperbacks, Golden Books, cloth books, board books—the larger the variety, the greater the sorting and classifying choices available for children as they play.

Contents

- books of various types
- toy cash register
- pads
- pencils
- markers
- receipt books
- folders or a poster for alphabetizing
- souvenirs and other items for selling in the store

Content Information

- Ask children if they have ever been to a bookstore with one of their family members. Encourage them to tell what they remember about the trip. Ask if any of them have purchased a book at a bookstore.
- Show a variety of books to your students and tell them that you can buy all types of books at a bookstore.
- Tell children that some people prefer to go to a library, because libraries allow readers to check out books for free instead of purchasing them.
- Give students opportunities to talk about their favorite books. Ask why they enjoy specific books.

Vocabulary Enrichment

- bookshelf
- spine
- pages
- author
- illustrator
- plot
- alphabet
- alphabetical order
- library
- foreign languages
- crafts
- travel
- self-help
- fiction
- nonfiction
- science fiction
- novelties
- librarian

Dramatic Play/Cooperation

- Children will discover their own approaches to developing bookstore play. Observe their play to suggest activities to enhance their learning and support cooperative behavior. For example, you can be a customer and ask for a specific book title to demonstrate how bookstores operate.

- Alphabetizing is a skill important to developing children's understanding of literacy that children can use during dramatic play. Encourage students to place their books on the shelf in alphabetical order. Use the alphabet dividers as an organizing feature for children, but be available to help children understand the reason why books should be organized by title.

Skills
Counting
- Ask students to count the number of books they have in their bookstore.

Sorting
- Suggest to students that they sort books into several categories (e.g., adult books, children's books about animals, counting or alphabet books). Allow them to sort with their own established standards.
- Books can further be sorted into categories within the categories. Children can sort books previously sorted into groups by content, fiction, or nonfiction.

Matching
- Matching cards can be prepared in several ways. One way is to write a key word onto a card and then have a matching card that has a picture on it. An example is to write the word *cat* on a card and then prepare a matching card that has a picture of a cat on it.
- Another way to prepare matching cards is to use a photo of the book cover on one card and another one that has the title printed.
- Students can also match book cover cards with characters from the book. If you use the cover from *Where the Wild Things Are* by Maurice Sendak, as an example, then you could copy one of the wild things on a matching card.

Initial consonant sounds
- Play a game with individual children or small groups asking them to find a book that has a word in its title that starts with a specific letter sound (e.g., the /c/ in *The Very Hungry Caterpillar* by Eric Carle).

Solving problems (riddles)
- Another game to play with individuals or small groups is to provide clues about a specific book for children to find. Say, "I'm thinking about a book that tells the story about a young boy who is trying to find a gift for his mother" as a clue for children to locate *Ask Mr. Bear* by Marjorie Flack. Add additional clues as needed until children find the book.

Writing
- Students can design book covers for some of the books in the store.
- Posters can be made advertising a new book in the store.

BOOKSTORE CENTER

- Place a table near the bookstore center for writing books. Provide paper, pencils, markers, crayons, and other supplies to encourage children to write stories and draw illustrations to accompany their work. The books can be added to the inventory of the store.

Money
- Prices can be added to the books using small sticky notes. With the addition of play money, students can purchase books.
- Play checkbooks or credit cards can be used to purchase books.

Other Ideas
- Prepare book cover puzzles by copying the covers (in color, preferably) and then cutting them into puzzle pieces. To protect them for the long term, laminate the pieces or cover them with clear contact paper.
- Copy book covers in varying sizes (small, medium, large) in color to allow children to match ones that are alike and put them in order sequentially. Glue the copied pictures onto large index cards and laminate them.
- In the art center, ask children to use art materials to develop their own posters representing books that are their favorites. You can write the titles of the books for the children or you can encourage children to try their own invented spelling. Hang their finished products in the bookstore center.
- Second graders will be able to do an in-depth study of a specific author. Survey your group to learn who their favorite author(s) are and encourage small-group or individual study. Remember to use the Internet as a source of information about current authors.

Book Connections
- Bauld, J. S. (2000). *We need librarians*. Minnetonka, MN: Capstone.
- Kimmel, E. A. (1992). *I took my frog to the library*. New York, NY: Puffin.
- Meister, C. (2011). *Tiny goes to the library*. New York, NY: Puffin.

Items That Families Might Donate or Loan to the Center
- outdated atlases or tourist guides
- children's books (marked with family names so that they may be returned)
- well-used children's books (to make puzzles or matching cards)
- souvenir items representing the community
- catalogues, brochures, or advertising flyers from area bookstores

SHOE STORE CENTER

One of the first stores that young children visit is the shoe store. Most children start each school year with a new pair of shoes. They are interested in seeing the new shoes of other children and in showing off their own. Because of their experiences with new shoes, this center will be very popular with the children.

The box design for the shoe store center does not need to be elaborate—in fact, you can enlist children's assistance in decorating the box. The first time you set up the center, prepare one side with a large sign that reads Shoe Store. Then ask children to find photographs of shoes in magazines or department store circular advertisements that they can cut out and glue or paste onto the remaining sides of the box. If your children are older and are capable of representative drawings, you might consider asking them to draw pictures of shoes onto the box. After their artistic endeavors are complete, you can protect the box for future use by adding clear contact paper to the sides.

Set up the shoe store center near open shelves in the classroom so that children will be able to display the shoes. If you provide time for dramatic play, you will need to use the cash register as well as pads and pencils for children's preparation of receipts for their customers.

Contents

- shoes of all types and sizes
- small empty shoe boxes for display purposes
- empty containers of shoe polish (cleaned well)
- shoe shine cloths
- small-sized stocking footlets (for trying on shoes)
- shoe catalogues
- photographs of shoes that are not available (e.g., dancing shoes, clown shoes)
- lacing frames (constructed so children can practice tying laces) or Velcro frames
- teacher-prepared shoe puzzles

Content Information

- With small groups of children, develop discussions about topics like why sandals are better to wear during the summer season; what materials shoes are made of (e.g., leather, canvas, patent leather, suede, rubber); and what are the different types of shoes available (e.g., ones with laces, others with straps, some with Velcro clasps or straps).
- When students wear new shoes to school, allow them to participate in new shoe show-and-tell.
- Find a pair of unusual shoes (e.g., ballet slippers, clogs, clown shoes) to show the class and ask children to talk about their unique features. Show shoes

that nurses wear and think about the reasons why medical professionals need special shoes.

Vocabulary Enrichment

- shoe store
- shoe sizes
- sandals
- tennis shoes
- sneakers
- loafers
- flip-flops
- clogs
- moccasins

- boots
- parts of shoes (toe, heel, sole, insole, instep)
- specialty shoes (nurse's shoes, military wear, dance shoes, clown shoes)
- shoe materials (leather, canvas, suede, patent leather)

Dramatic Play/Cooperation

- Provide opportunities for children to pretend to run a shoe store by displaying pairs of shoes on open shelves. Children can sell shoes to their customers and write out receipts for them.
- Have shoe boxes available for students to use in their pretend play.

Skills

Measuring

- Show students how to use a shoe as a nonstandard measure and then measure various surfaces in the classroom (e.g., length of a table, how high a shelf is, how wide the door is). Record their measurements on a classroom chart.
- Provide rulers for standard measuring of the shoes.

Graphing

- Organize a graphing experience with children to determine which type of shoe is worn most often in school.

Understanding size

- Discover the median size of the children's shoes in your classroom (for first and second graders).
- Help individual children trace their baby shoes and the shoes they wear currently. Talk about the differences in size and width. You can also compare children's shoes with adult shoes using the same approach.

Matching
- Put numerous pairs of shoes in a large pile and request that students match them.

Sorting
- Ask students to sort shoes by type (e.g., those with straps, those with laces).

Ordering
- Find several shoes that are various colors and ask children to put them in order from lightest to darkest.
- Shoes can also be ordered by length and/or weight (using a scale).

Money
- Order forms can be provided for the catalogue or online department of the store. Use catalogues from stores and make copies of the order forms. Advanced learners can figure out the cost of shipping.

Other Ideas

- Develop shoe puzzles by preparing shoe shapes of different colors and cutting them into four or five pieces. Laminate the puzzle pieces to keep them for future use and save them in Ziploc bags so children can have ready access to them.
- Ask students to trace the shoes they wear to school and "write" a story about them (accept their scribbles, invented writing, or whatever marks they make on paper as writing).
- Ask children to think of words that begin with the /sh/ sound and write them on a large chart on or a word wall. This activity would be particularly good for first and second graders or for children who love challenges.
- Use an old pair of shoes (sneakers would be a good choice) and allow children to dip them into tempera paint to make shoeprints on large pieces of paper.
- Set up a section of the art center to give children an opportunity to polish pairs of shoes. Some children would enjoy using markers to decorate old canvas sneakers.
- Work with students to invent a song about shoes. Here is a possibility:

    Shoes (Tune: "Skip to My Lou")
    Shoes, shoes, see our fancy shoes;
    Shoes, shoes, see our fancy shoes;
    Shoes, shoes, see our fancy shoes;
    The shoes we're wearing today.

- Second graders will be able to do an in-class research study to determine the brand name of shoes that is most often worn by the class. Introduce the bar graph concept, so students can view the results of their data collection.

SHOE STORE CENTER

SHOE STORE CENTER

Book Connections

- Asher, S. (2001). *Stella's dancing days*. New York, NY: Harcourt.
- Crews, N. (2004). *The neighborhood mother goose*. New York, NY: Greenwillow.
- Littlesugar, A. (2006). *Clown child*. New York, NY: Penguin.
- Miller, M. (1991). *Whose shoe?* New York, NY: Greenwillow.
- Ransom, C. (1995). *The big green pocketbook*. New York, NY: HarperCollins.

Items That Families Might Donate or Loan to the Center

- specialty shoes that they are willing to loan to the classroom (e.g., dancing shoes, military boots, nurse's shoes, cowboy boots; have them to mark their names on the shoes so that they can be easily returned)

- shoes from their child's infancy or early years to use for comparison purposes

BANK CENTER

Banks, vaults, money, and coins all have appeal to children. This center will give them the opportunity to use these materials in meaningful activities that will allow them to practice skills that they have previously learned in new and exciting ways.

The box will be the bank's vault. With the box top on the box, stand the box on one of its short sides with the top facing you. Cut a large door that is almost the size of the top. Have it open to the right into the box. Attach a handle on the door, reinforced by a thin piece of wood on the back (or use several layers of corrugated cardboard). Buy a combination lock and cut a hole in the door that will be a very snug fit for it to slide into. Secure the lock from the back using duct tape. Make a shelf in the safe by taking a corrugated cardboard box and cutting a piece that is the width of the box plus another 20 inches. Fold down 10 inches on each side of the piece. This will be the support for the shelf. Slide it into the vault. A teller's window may be added to the center by using a smaller box without a top. Use of a smaller box will allow for the teller's window to be stored inside the bank vault. With the box flat on the table, cut out one long side of the box completely. On the other long side, cut a window from the top, leaving about 3 inches on each side. A table or child's desk will be needed for the teller's window. Set this box on the desk.

If the size of your classroom permits, use another desk or table to hold pens and the deposit slips and counter checks.

Contents

- bank counter checks and deposit slips (create and print these from the computer)
- date stamp
- cash drawer with paper money and coins
- calculator
- paper
- pens

- coin rolls
- extra play money coins
- generous supply of real pennies (for rolling)
- large stacks of play dollars
- large canvas sack for coins (to place in the bottom of the vault)
- a number word chart (for filling out checks)

Content Information

- Begin by asking the children to tell you what they know about banks. Correct any misunderstandings that the children have. Some children may not have any experience with a bank. Explain how a bank works and why people use banks.
- Read a book that explains how banks function.

BANK CENTER

- Ask your local bank for permission to take pictures of the inside of their bank and use these pictures in your discussion with the children.
- Explain the vocabulary words appropriate for your grade level (some of the words listed below are more appropriate for older or gifted children).

Vocabulary Enrichment

- vault
- safe
- deposit
- bank teller
- safety deposit boxes
- check
- interest/interest rate
- statement
- withdrawal
- deposit slip
- void
- overdrawn
- mortgage
- loan
- checking and savings accounts
- credit and debit cards
- online banking
- balance
- fees
- credit rating
- ATM machine
- certificates of deposit
- FDIC insured

Dramatic Play/Cooperation

- Introduce the center and show the children all of the different items that you have in the center. Demonstrate to the children how a bank scenario might go. Pretend you have a check to cash or money to deposit and so you go up to the teller with your request. If a child has never been in a bank, she will need this example before she can understand how to play bank. Many children from low-income families don't use banks. Other children may have been in the car and gone through the drive-through, but never been inside the bank.
- Show how you have to stop at the table and fill out a deposit form for your money.
- Ask for change from your check with specific types of money: "I need $10 bills, please."

Skills

Sorting

- Using the cash drawer, have students sort all of the money into the bill and coin slots.

Counting and adding

- The children can count five groups of 10 pennies, and then roll the pennies into the coin holders.
- Pretend rolls of dimes, nickels, and quarters can be counted using skip counting.

Adding and subtracting

- Using checks of varying amounts, the children can fill out a deposit slip and add the total deposit. Amounts will depend upon the skill level of the children, but the teacher can have deposit totals that are very easy to add and those that are more challenging.
- Laminate "loan records" balance sheets. Children can add an entry for a payment with an erasable marker and subtract it from the amount owed. Bank records showing deposits to savings accounts can be added.

Counting change

- Using small coin purses with varying amounts of change, have students count the change in each purse and match the purse to a card with the same amount.

Making change

- Children can use premade checks with specific amounts already on the checks to count out the correct change. For example, the check might read $0.57.

Sequencing coins by date

- Have pennies or nickels from different years. Place the coins in two-by-two holders. Show the children where the dates can be found. Have them put the coins in chronological order.

Reading mint marks and dates

- Have two-by-two coin holders marked with information such as "penny 1989 D." The students will need to be shown where the letters D and P are located on the coins. D means it was minted at the Denver Mint; P stands for the Philadelphia Mint. They will find the penny and place it in the correct holder.

Writing

- Students can fill out blank checks as part of pretend play. Older and gifted children can practice writing the checks correctly, including using the number words. Checks could be premade with the amount written in using numerals and then laminated. The children could then use a dry-erase marker and fill in the number words to match the numeral.

BANK CENTER

Other Ideas

- Save the ads from the newspaper for ordering specialized checks and show them to the children. Have the children design their own specialized checks.
- Show students the form for opening a checking account. Have them fill in the information.
- Invite a bank manager to come visit your classroom and explain all of the jobs that people have in a bank.
- Look for ads in the newspaper for interest rates on certificates of deposit and bring in several with different interest rates. Have students use the Internet to figure the amount they will earn on their money at the different banks.
- Show the children a bank statement and canceled checks. Talk about why it is important to know how much money you have in your account and what happens if you write a check and don't have the money in the account. Have children balance very simple statements.
- Invite a coin collector to your class.
- Have books on the history of coins and coin collecting available in the classroom.

Book Connections

- Brown, M. (2004). *Arthur breaks the bank*. New York, NY: Random House.
- Mayer, G., & Mayer, M. (2001). *Just a piggy bank*. New York, NY: Golden Books.
- Smith, K. (2008). *Let's go to the bank*. New York, NY: Rosen.

Items That Families Might Donate or Loan to the Center

- credit card applications that arrive with a hard plastic sample credit card (use the card as a pretend card and the applications in play or to be filled out by the children when they "apply" for a credit card)
- pennies (for counting and rolling purposes)
- canvas bank bags and zippered bags printed with bank names
- two-by-two holders for the coins

OFFICE CENTER

Children are familiar with the school's office, even if they have never been in any other office. They see the secretary, the boss (principal), the office machines, filing cabinets, and papers. Visiting the office will provide them with information about offices in general and will assist in their dramatic play.

The box representing the office center box should serve as a paper box. Most offices have reams of paper stacked in boxes in supply storerooms, so leave the box as it is. Retain identifying information on the box to add to its authenticity. Pattern your office center to resemble offices your children know. If your students have family members who work at state, county, or city agencies, plan contents and activities that demonstrate familiar offices. University and community college offices also have unique features, so think about your children's understanding of office operations. If you live in a city, your students may be aware of corporations and the corporate structure. Talk to your children's families to gain insight about the types of offices that need to be represented during your study and plan your office study accordingly.

Place the office center near the classroom computer station. You will need additional tables for dramatic play and a small file cabinet, if you can locate one in your school. If your school has a computer lab, consider using the office center study to launch an interest in children's computer opportunities.

Contents

- pencils
- pencil holder
- pencil sharpener
- collection of pens with business logos
- Rolodex
- a telephone book (an outdated book is acceptable)
- clock
- a desk calendar
- glasses frames (minus lenses)
- stenographer pads
- an old coffeepot (with the cord removed)
- a snap-on tie or two
- junk mail
- an old typewriter (either manual or electric)
- additional keyboards (for children's practice)
- stapler and staples
- paper clip holder
- one or more toy telephones
- an answering machine (does not have to be operational)
- at least one calculator
- at least one ream of paper
- stamp pad

71

OFFICE CENTER

Content Information

- As you introduce the office center, think about taking your students on a mini-field trip to the school's office. Point out features of the office, such as the telephone and voice mail system, copier, file cabinets, desk, wastebasket, storeroom or supply cabinet, paper shredder, computer, calculator, and whatever else you deem necessary to observe.

- Show children samples of letterhead stationery and envelopes. Ask them if they want to name the classroom office and prepare stationery representing the office. Facilitate a brainstorming session, and then have a stamp made for them to prepare stationery and envelopes with letterhead markings. For example, if they choose to call the office Mrs. Payne's Kindergarten Office, you can go to an office supply store and have a stamp made for a fairly inexpensive cost.

- For some groups of students, consider introducing terms such as *corporation* or *company*. You may want to talk about various departments and offices that exist within the corporate structure. Discuss that companies need employees who can make sure that the public knows about their function (marketing department), other employees who sell products made by the company (sales team), and others who make sure that the company is making money (finance department). Older children are able to acquire limited knowledge about investments and may want to know about the stock market.

Vocabulary Enrichment

- secretary
- receptionist
- chief executive officer
- president
- vice president
- boss
- office manager
- accountant
- bookkeeper
- clerical assistance
- file clerk
- mail room and mail room clerk
- employees
- mail delivery
- incoming and outgoing mail
- keyboard
- coffee break
- sales team
- marketing department
- finance department
- investments
- stock market
- paper shredder

Dramatic Play/Cooperation

- Once students recognize the function of an office (gained from their mini-field trip), the classroom set up should encourage office play. At first, you can serve as the boss, telling children the tasks that need to be done by a certain time of the day.

- When it's time for coffee break (snack time), talk to students about what this means and why employees need opportunities to rest for a few minutes.

- Introduce the typewriter and talk to children about its similarity to the computer keyboard. If numerous students want to use the typewriter, bring in additional keyboards (borrowed from families) for children's pretend play.

- Place a stapler and staples in the center. Put some junk mail in the center for stapling purposes so that your paper supplies are not wasted.

- Talk to children about the secretarial responsibility of recording incoming telephone calls in a telephone log. Students can share their home phone numbers with one another in this pretend experience.

- Interested children will gravitate to the office center time and time again as they explore the typewriter, participate in various writing experiences, and sort mail for distribution to others in the classroom.

Skills

Fine-motor development
- Students who have never used a pencil sharpener will take pride in sharpening pencils for use in the office center.
- Give children boxes of paper clips so that they can hook them together into paper clip chains. Periodically ask children to count the number of paper clips on their chains. Individual children may find satisfaction in counting by 10s. Measure the finished product so children can tell their families about their accomplishment.

Counting
- Talk to students about taking inventory. Discuss why taking stock of office equipment and supplies helps determine whether the business or company is making money. Ask children to count office supplies or equipment. Suggest that they prepare a chart showing what is available in the office. Also, recommend that they count the office equipment.

Addition or multiplication
- Show students how to use a calculator to add numerals. Second graders can try multiplication using the calculator. Remind children that offices need mathematical information that requires both of these processes. Tell them that this is one of the responsibilities of the finance department.

Graphing
- Ask children to take a survey of their family members to learn the variety of modes of transportation they use to get to work. For small communities, workers usually drive a car, walk, take a bus, or ride bicycles to work.

OFFICE CENTER

In larger communities, workers may use car pools, a van pool, or trains and subway systems to get to work. Use a bar graph to display the data that were collected.

Telling time

- Talk to students about the 9–5 workday. Using a commercially prepared clock, ask children to move the hands to represent specific times, such as coffee break (10 a.m.), lunch (noon), and quitting time (5 p.m.). Tell students that some employees work with alternate schedules and explain what this means for offices in your community.

Alphabetization

- Using a Rolodex organizer, ask students to write their first names on individual cards to place into the Rolodex. Show them the alphabetic inserts that will allow them to place their card in the appropriate place. Periodically take out all of the name cards and ask children to reinsert the cards in the correct section of the Rolodex.
- If you have children who have names that begin with the same letter, teach children how to alphabetize in each section using letters in the second and third positions.
- Provide a telephone book and ask individual children to find someone's phone number using their alphabetization skills.

Writing

- Describe the "taking dictation" process to children. Tell children that bosses sometimes verbalize the letters they want to write to their secretaries, who then type the letters. Have a dictation session with small groups of students by speaking numerals or single words for them to write onto pads of paper. Older children will be able to take your dictation role once they are familiar with the experience.
- Tell students that office employees often prepare reports for their bosses. The survey of modes of transportation or the accounting of office inventory described previously can serve as information that children can use to prepare a report. When each report is prepared, children can share the results with the center director or their principal.
- Specify the marketing department's function in making brochures about the company and selecting logos. Ask children to write blurbs about the office they have developed and find a logo to match the office name. Here are a few examples you can give them for the writing and logo development activity: Eagle Copy Center, Lone Tree Furniture Store, Jumping Jack Gym, Brown's Office Supply, Able Glass and Mirror Store, and King's Candy Store.

Reading
- File junk mail in file cabinet folders by alphabetizing mail pieces by business names. Not only are students "reading" the mail, they are alphabetizing what they are reading.
- Cut out and collect corporate logo designs from various products and display them in plastic dividers to make a logo album. Use logos of corporations that appeal to children (e.g., sodas, drink mixes, cereals, various candy and gum wrappers, soaps). Work with children individually and in small groups to figure out how many children recognize. This is an example of children reading environmental print.
- A collection of pens from local businesses or corporations that have names on them can also challenge students to read print in their environment.

Throwing
- Suggest to younger children that they do a wastebasket toss. Make paper balls by wadding junk mail into ball-like masses and, and standing behind a predetermined line, toss them into the wastebasket. As students gain expertise with this game, move the line farther away from the wastebasket to make the experience more challenging. Make sure students know tossing paper into the wastebasket is not appropriate outside of the center.

Other Ideas
- Show children what a paper shredder can do. Students can glue shredded paper onto construction paper to make interesting art designs. Use the artwork as decoration for the office center. Explain the safety rules for using paper shredders.
- Tell children what the phrase "brown-bagging it" means. Ask if any of their family members take their lunches to work. Provide bread, sandwich spreads, lunch meat, and other foodstuffs so children can make a brown bag lunch. Place the sandwiches into sandwich bags and put them in brown bags for lunch later in the day.

Book Connections
- Cronin, D. (2000). *Click, clack, moo: Cows that type*. New York, NY: Simon & Schuster.
- Estes, E. (2000). *Pinky pye*. New York, NY: Harcourt.

OFFICE CENTER

OFFICE CENTER

Items That Families Might Donate or Loan to the Center

- junk mail
- pens with business or corporation logos on them

- discarded keyboards
- old desk accessories

POST OFFICE CENTER

One of the first field trips in early childhood classrooms is a visit to the local post office. Introducing a post office center after this field trip will greatly increase the children's enjoyment of this center.

Little preparation is needed to turn a box into the post office counter. This box will be turned upside down and the bottom of the box will become the counter. Print or glue the words Post Office on the long side of the box. Decorate the box with a picture of a flag and red, white, and blue stripes. Make a door cut on the other long side (see Figure 1). This will create a compartment for storing forms, a date stamp and inkpad, stamps, and a cash drawer. The teacher might decide to use a classroom desk for the post office counter. In this case, the box can be turned into boxes for the sorting of mail. Long narrow boxes may be purchased, glued together and stacked inside the box, or a box that contained bottles of wine may be obtained from a store and fitted into the paper box. This usually leaves a section on the side that can hold other supplies.

The teacher can pick up copies of various forms at a post office to use as samples for creating forms for the classroom. Different colored paper for forms makes them more realistic and appealing. A date stamp, a canceled stamp, and an inkpad will be enticing to the children. The canceled stamp can be purchased at any store that makes specialty stamps.

A postal scale, tape measure, and boxes of various sizes and weights need to be prepared. Padded envelopes and flat envelopes of differing sizes will be needed. Some can be "sold" in the post office and others can be placed in the writing center for the students to use for their letters. Stamps can be made by taking return address stickers and cutting off the name so that only the picture remains.

Contents

- post office forms
- date stamp
- canceled stamp
- inkpad
- postal scale
- tape measure
- boxes
- envelopes
- stamps (stickers or labels)

Content Information

- Most students will have some rudimentary understanding of the post office, but it will probably be limited to the job of mail carrier and delivering letters. Talk about what happens from the time the letter is dropped into a mailbox and before the mail carrier actually delivers a letter. Show the chil-

POST OFFICE CENTER

dren a correctly addressed envelope and talk about the importance of all the various parts. For instance, why would you need a return address on your envelope? Show the children information about weight and size restrictions on packages. Brainstorm the types of materials that would not be good to mail, and visit the United States Postal Service website to see the list of prohibited materials.

- Show various types of postage: stamps, metered mail, and printed postage. Talk about the purpose of canceling postage and the postmark.
- Introduce the postal scale and show the children how to read the scale. Have a chart that shows the price of a stamp for the first ounce and then the price for each additional ounce.

Vocabulary Enrichment

- Forever Stamp
- first class
- postmark
- overnight
- forward
- junk mail
- metered mail
- postal regulations
- oversize
- legible

- prohibited
- USPS
- change of address
- zip codes
- track
- Postmaster General
- international postage
- priority
- certified
- registered

Dramatic Play/Cooperation

- After the discussion of the postal service, introduce the center and the different activities that are available. Brainstorm with the children ways that they could play with the center and how they could use materials in the writing center in their play.
- If students have cubbies or tubs with their names on them, they could use these as the mailboxes for letters written in class.
- A visor and large bag can be added to the center. This would allow the children to play the role of mail carrier.

Skills

Counting

- Children can count stamps and put them into groups (use small numbers for younger students all the way up to groups of 100).

Measuring
- Students can use the measuring tape to measure and record the length, width, and height of packages of various sizes. Use the post office guidelines for mailing packages and have some of the packages oversized. These will either be refused or charged extra because of their size.
- Have the children figure out the correct postage to place on packages of various weights. Students can match up preprinted stamps with the costs of mailing the packages.

Estimation
- Have the children estimate one-ounce amounts of various materials and then check their estimate. Have them place the material in an envelope and weigh it again.

Writing
- Encourage students to write letters to each other. Have a dictionary available for them to use to check their spelling and to look up words.
- Children can use the computer to type letters and practice using spell and grammar checkers.
- Have index cards available with the students' addresses on them. By writing letters to their parents and addressing the envelopes, the children can work on learning their addresses.

Reading and classifying
- Bring in an assortment of junk mail and have the children classify the mail.
- Have the students write down differences between the address and postage on junk mail and regular mail.

Sorting
- Using premade envelopes, have the children sort the envelopes into boxes. Prekindergarten children can sort by color or shape on the envelope; older students can sort by zip code, state, or some other criteria.

Computer use, history, and research
- Have older children use the Internet to research the history of the postal service. Let them prepare a presentation for the class and make posters to display their information.
- Have students look up zip codes for various addresses of businesses in different cities of your state.

Other Ideas
- Give the children a sheet of small labels and have them design different stamps for the post office.
- Have students visit http://usps.com and see all that you can do online now (e.g., print online postage, change address, find zip codes, track packages).

POST OFFICE CENTER

POST OFFICE CENTER

- Take a field trip to a large, central post office. Your students will be able to see how machines do the sorting of the mail, why it is important to address your mail in a legible manner, and all of the steps mail goes through before it even is placed in a mail carrier's bag for delivery.
- Find another class in another state, and contact it about becoming pen pals with your class.
- Invite a stamp collector to the classroom to talk about stamp collecting and show off his or her stamps.

Book Connections

- Frederick, D. (2002). *How it happens at the post office.* Minneapolis, MN: Oliver Press.
- Gibbons, G. (1986). *The post office book: Mail and how it moves.* New York, NY: HarperCollins.

Items That Families Might Donate or Loan to the Center

- envelopes from bills (without the bills included)
- junk mail
- envelopes from personal mail
- large manila envelopes and overnight envelopes
- return address labels that include a picture
- mismatched envelopes

LAUNDROMAT CENTER

Washing clothes is a common activity in every household. Parents who use laundromats often take their children with them. The children are familiar with the routines of sorting clothes, putting money in the washers, adding soap, and drying the clothes. They may even be familiar with change machines. Children who go with their parents to the laundromat will have more knowledge about this center than children whose parents do the wash at home.

You can choose to paint the box for your laundromat center or not. Many laundromats (sometimes referred to as washaterias) have white washing machines and dryers, so having a white box is appropriate. Your box lid can serve as the door to the washer, and cutting a door inside the lid with a sharp knife should be fairly easy. Leave about a 5-inch margin and cut only three sides (at the top, on one side, and at the bottom). Glue the lid to the box, and use the "door" as the opening to the box. If you want a second box to represent a dryer, you can follow similar directions to make another box.

Paint a rectangle on the box lid to serve as a coin collection site. Cut a hole in the rectangle that will allow coins to pass through into the box. If you make a second box for a dryer, you will need to a coin receptacle for it as well.

You may want to add a window in the door for pretend viewing of the clothes that are washing, so cut out a round piece in the middle of the door and tape strong cellophane on the inside. If you follow this plan, please recognize that you diminish the box's durability. The cellophane will tear easily with the normal wear and tear of children's play, so be prepared to replace it from year to year.

Position the laundromat center near a low table with several chairs placed around it. You may want to have a small tub of water and liquid detergent available to encourage children to wash the doll clothes in the classroom. They will also need another tub of water to rinse the clothes. Many of the items you will use for this center will need to be gathered from your home instead of being stored from year to year.

Contents

- small laundry basket
- a few empty boxes of detergent
- an empty bottle of fabric softener
- fabric softener sheets
- a detergent measuring cup

- clothes that families may have donated to the center
- play coins
- photographs of laundromats children may frequent

Content Information

- Talk to children about why they might need to visit a laundromat (e.g., some families do not own washers and dryers, the family appliances are broken, they have large items that need to be washed).
- Identify students whose families visit laundromats on a regular basis, allowing them to dictate a story to you that you can share with the entire group. The story, referred to as a language experience activity, should tell about their trips to the laundromat. Write the sentences on a large chart tablet. Add a photograph of a laundromat to the story and display it in the classroom.
- If your school has a washer and dryer, take the children to observe them in action. Taking this mini-field trip in small groups will give children a better opportunity to observe the appliances. If you choose to wash doll clothing, you may choose to dry them in the school's dryer.

Vocabulary Enrichment

- laundry
- detergent
- fabric softener
- fabric softener sheets
- laundromat/washateria
- coins or quarters
- washer
- dryer
- folding table
- wash cycle
- rinse cycle
- drying cycle
- stains
- stubborn spots
- bleach
- stain removers

Dramatic Play/Cooperation

- If you have provided tubs of water, students can wash the classroom dolls' clothing. You will need to supervise so that children will understand the importance of rinsing the clothes after they are washed. You will also need to find a spot in the classroom or on the playground for the clothes to dry.
- Bring in an iron and child-sized ironing board so children can pretend to iron the clothes they have washed.

Skills

Measuring

- Discuss why it is necessary to measure laundry detergent and fabric softener. Have several cups available for children to use for experimentation. Fill empty detergent boxes with sand and fabric softener bottles with water to facilitate the play. You will probably want to use the classroom water and sand tables for this experience.

Folding
- Introduce the concept of folding clothes for storage to students.

Sorting
- Talk to children about sorting clothes into whites and colors. Explain why colored clothes should not be washed with white clothes.
- Encourage children to sort clothes after they are washed and dried, explaining that they are easier to return to their storage shelves and drawers if they are sorted. If you have a variety of clothing (e.g., for adults, children, infants), sorting the items should present a challenge to your group.

Differentiating odors
- Place small tubs of dirty laundry and clean laundry side by side near the laundromat center so students can compare the smells. Towels and washcloths are good choices for these tubs.

Tracing and cutting
- Provide pretend coins for children to trace onto construction paper or index cards and cut out. They can use their completed coins in their dramatic play.

Matching
- Prepare several matching cards showing coins in various configurations. Use pretend money to encourage students to match the configurations on blank cards. Older children will be able to prepare their own matching cards for other children in the classroom.

Measuring
- Save liquid detergent containers of various sizes. Black out the label that tells the amount of liquid. Have students use measuring cups and water to determine how much liquid each container holds.
- Using detergent containers of various sizes, fill or partially fill them with water. Have the children use a scale and weigh each container. They can record the weights and order the containers from lightest to heaviest.

Experimenting
- With small samples of different detergents and small samples of cloth with dirt, grass stains, grease, and lipstick, have the children test the detergents to see which one works best on which stain.
- Using different detergents, have students experiment to see which one makes the most suds. Use the Internet to determine why suds are important.
- Students can compare detergent that is concentrated to one that is not, then report on their findings.

LAUNDROMAT CENTER

LAUNDROMAT CENTER

Other Ideas

- Sing the familiar song "This Is the Way We Wash Our Clothes" with children at some point during the study:

    This is the way we wash our clothes, wash our clothes, wash our clothes,
    This is the way we wash our clothes, so early in the morning.

- Use a clean table in the classroom to mix up detergent and water to form a soapy substance. Children can use the suds to make pictures on the table or on large pieces of construction paper.
- Provide a box of fabric softener sheets for children's art, allowing them to make interesting designs on them with markers.
- Students can also prepare a fabric softener sheet as a gift for the family by rolling it up and tying it with a piece of yarn. Teachers may need to assist the children with tying the yarn.
- Second graders will be able to conduct a survey of their families' choices for favorite detergents, fabric softeners, and spot removers. They can also do in-class research to determine which of a selection of three or four spot remover products actually achieves the best results.

Book Connections

- Bond, M. (1981). *Paddington at the laundromat.* Los Angeles, CA: Price Stern Sloan.
- Garland, S. (2009). *Doing the washing.* London, England: Frances Lincoln Children's Books.
- Rey, M., & Shalleck, A. (1987). *Curious George goes to the laundromat.* New York, NY: Houghton Mifflin.

Items That Families Might Donate or Loan to the Center

- empty detergent boxes and bottles
- empty fabric softener bottles
- unused clothing

PHARMACY CENTER

Children often go to the pharmacy with their parents. Parents may be picking up a prescription, stopping in to have photos developed, or buying cough medicine. The more familiar a child is with a real pharmacy, the more complex their dramatic play will be. Planning a pharmacy center implies that teachers will need to make decisions about the messages they are sending to children about drugs and taking medicines during this particular study. Consider talking to children about the need to use medicines that are prescribed by their doctors and using over-the-counter medicines that are appropriate for their age. Be prepared to talk about the sign for poison as well. Discussing with families what their preferences are will lead to a better understanding about how the topic should be used in the classroom.

The box design for the pharmacy center should be fairly simple, perhaps displaying the mortar and pestle logo used by many pharmacies on one side of the box. The skull and crossbones danger sign could be included on the opposite of the box, providing an opportunity to talk about what the symbol means. Most paper boxes are white, so affix the logos with tape or glue for easy construction.

Once the box is complete, it can serve as a counter for sales or the pharmacist can use it for preparing prescriptions. You'll probably need a toy cash register and telephone to promote dramatic play, but these items can be borrowed from existing classroom centers. Occasionally, students may use the box as a storage space for medicines.

Contents

- cotton balls
- tongue depressors
- boxes of tissue
- empty medicine bottles (cleaned thoroughly)
- empty containers of over-the-counter products (e.g., pain relievers, cough syrups, antacids), also cleaned thoroughly
- buttons or beads (for pills)
- cellophane or plastic gloves (some children are allergic to latex)
- gauze
- bandages
- stethoscope
- get well cards or blank floral cards
- toy doctor's kit
- pharmacist's jacket (or a white shirt)
- prescription pads (or just blank pads of paper)
- small trays for holding "medicines" while they are being counted for prescriptions
- toy telephone
- small plastic baskets for holding prescriptions until patients pick up their medicine
- toy cash register

PHARMACY CENTER

Content Information

- Talk to children about pharmacies and what they are. Show photographs of pharmacies in the community (if you have them).
- Ask students to tell about a time their family needed to go to a pharmacy to pick up medication. Ask if they met the pharmacist.
- Talk to children about the importance of only taking medicines that have been prescribed by their doctors or purchased over the counter by their families.

Dramatic Play/Cooperation

- Provide opportunities for students to pretend to be pharmacists and pharmacist assistants. Join their play, modeling how customers call in and pick up their prescriptions.
- Show children how to write patients' names on labels to place on medicine bottles.
- Demonstrate how baskets are used to hold medications until patients come in to pick up their prescriptions.

Vocabulary Enrichment

- pharmacy
- pharmacist
- pharmacist assistant
- prescription
- prescription pad
- medicine
- dose or dosage
- diagnosis
- germs
- tongue depressor

Skills

Counting

- Using beads and a tongue depressor, demonstrate how pharmacists count pills to put into medicine bottles. Challenge older students to count the beads by twos or even by fives. Have bottles premarked with numerals (10, 20, 30) so children will know how far they need to count. Some students will enjoy counting to 50 or 100.

Ordering

- Ask children to order bottles by size from smallest to largest.
- Provide packages or bottles with varying amounts of pills and have students order them from fewest to most pills.

Estimating and counting
- Prepare at least two medicine bottles with varying numbers of pills in them. Ask individual students to estimate which of the bottles has the *most* medicine or the *least* medicine. Then encourage children to count the contents of each to discover if they were correct in their estimation.

Sorting
- Use different colors or sizes of beads or buttons in the medicine bottles. Ask students to take out the contents of each bottle and sort the items by color or size.

Writing, reading, and alphabetizing
- Prepare prescriptions that the pharmacist will need to prepare. Use blank paper and large packing tape to make reusable labels on the bottles. The students will read the prescription, count the correct number of pills into the bottle, and use a dry erase marker to write the name and the number of pills on the label. The prescriptions can then be filed in alphabetical order in a file box.
- Provide blank prescription pads for the children to use to write prescriptions.
- Have a box of index cards with various descriptions of illnesses and the age of the person. Also have empty bottles or boxes of different types of medicines. The students will read the card and place it with the appropriate medicine box or bottle. For example, a card with "This child is 2 years old and is running a fever" might go with baby aspirin.
- Have children compare brand-name vitamins to store-brand ones. What is the difference in the vitamins and their costs?

Mathematics computation
- Provide several sizes of vitamin bottles with their costs listed and have children figure out the best buy.
- Save sale ads and have students compare the cost of items on a list if they bought them on sale versus not on sale. Be sure the ads say, "Save $_____ when you buy _____."

Measuring
- Have the children read information on prepared index cards, go to the pharmacy, and choose the appropriate product. For example, a card could say "You were cut by glass and your wound is 2" by 1/4" in size. Find the best size bandage for your wound."

Other Ideas
- Students can use modeling clay to make small round or oval-shaped pills to place in medicine bottles when they play.

- Talk to children about covering their noses and mouths when they sneeze to avoid spreading germs. Then ask them to draw pictures of themselves sneezing and glue a tissue over their nose and mouth for a classroom bulletin board (or to take home).
- Set up a get well card station to allow children to make cards or write cards for their sick friends. Remind children that when people are ill, they go to a pharmacy to get their medications if the doctor has written a prescription for them.
- Bring in drugstore newspaper inserts and ask children to cut out the items that might go into a bathroom medicine cabinet. They can glue them onto a poster prepared to look like a medicine cabinet. Give children a chance to tell why they made the choices they made.
- Challenge second graders to read the directions on medications and ask them to tell you what they mean.

Book Connections
- London, J. (2004). *Froggy goes to the doctor*. New York, NY: Puffin.
- Thorpe, K. (2003). *Ah–choo!* New York, NY: Simon Spotlight/Nickelodeon.

Items That Families Might Donate or Loan to the Center
- empty medicine bottles and other containers that have been cleaned thoroughly
- pharmacy sacks and medicine label descriptions
- blank note pads to be used as prescription pads
- get well or blank cards

Chapter 8 Specialty Store Theme Centers

Children's interest in their immediate surroundings, their emerging understanding of their community, and what they observe when they visit an area mall are the rationale for the centers described in this section. This chapter focuses on stores and businesses that interest children but ones that they may not visit often. Center experiences based on specialty stores provide advantageous teaching situations to build children's skills and expand their knowledge base.

As you organize the center boxes described in this section, remember that children's play and interactions with others are critical for conceptual development and practice with skills that are essential for their overall learning. Give children time to acquire knowledge and apply skills in the nonthreatening approach to learning they need.

CARD AND PARTY SHOP CENTER

Children can relate to this store because they usually have experience with birthday parties. The materials will encourage them to plan a party in the classroom and then go to the store to buy the materials for the party.

This box will be transformed into a rack that will hold an assortment of cards for the center. With the box bottom sitting on a table, make cuts from the top edge to the bottom on each side of one long side. This will free one long side so it can now be folded down. Now cut along the bottom of each of the short sides and fold the end pieces out in a 45-degree angle. This leaves only the remaining long side connected to the bottom of the box (three open sides cut; see Figure 3).

Make the pockets on the two sides and the back by using strips of poster board about 2 inches wide. Make the pockets in three sections—one for each side and one for the back. Use contact paper to tape these to the back and sides. Clear pockets can be made using only contact paper and folding it over on itself where the pocket will be. A lower level and upper level pocket will fit. The results resemble a pocket chart. The sections can be labeled on the pockets. You might have one section for birthday cards, another for get well cards, and the third for other occasion cards. Place the cards inside the strips. Place the box on the edge of a desk or a table with the long side folded over the edge. This side can be decorated with the name "Card and Party Shop." You can use scrapbook decorations to enhance the appearance of the sign.

The top of the box can be divided into sections with cardboard dividers to make bins for the various party supplies. A trip to a card and party store can give the teacher many ideas about how to arrange the different items that are found in such stores. Buy items that are cheap and have several in the bag, but also make sure not to buy things children will put their mouths on, like whistles and flutes. Each bin can then be labeled with sticky notes as to what the content should be. By using sticky notes instead of actually writing on the dividers, you can constantly change the positions and add or subtract items from the store. When folding this center back up for storage, you will probably want to secure each cut side with a single piece of masking tape. The top of the box will hold the sides in place.

Contents

- birthday candles
- cups
- napkins
- small plates
- plastic spoons and forks
- playing cards, Old Maid, Go Fish, and other card games
- a variety of greeting cards
- paper from the writing center, stamps, and ink pads (to make cards)
- cash register
- play money
- order pads
- purses
- sacks

Content Information

- Talk to the students about parties. What are some of the things that they remember? Explain that card and party shops carry a wide assortment of party favors, special decorations, and matching plates and cups, in addition to cards for all occasions. These stores have much more variety than you could find in a grocery store or discount store.
- Have students name different events that might occur in which someone would want to send a card to someone. The card and party shop would have cards for these occasions, plus cards for other special occasions.
- Discuss the concept of store inventory with the children. Using concrete examples, explain why stores have to take inventory of their stock and discuss why this is important. Ask them if they have ever gone to the store to buy several of the same type of item. What would happen if you went to the party store to buy favors and they didn't have enough for your party?

Vocabulary Enrichment

- party favors
- matching plates and cups
- sympathy cards
- retirement cards
- invitations

- helium balloons
- special occasions
- streamers
- inventory
- stock

Dramatic Play/Cooperation

- Introduce the center to the children and explain all of the different areas. Have a child role-play with you so you can demonstrate how the center can be used.
- Tell your students that they can make invitations in the writing center for parties, and they can use the dolls and the home center to have their party.

Skills

Reading

- Using the special occasion cards will encourage the children to read the messages inside in order to pick the appropriate card.
- The store clerk will have to read the cards in order to restock the shelves.
- Party items will be sorted into groups and placed according to labels that are in the different bins.

Writing
- Provide access to the art and writing center and paper, stamps, and inkpads for the children to make their own cards and invitations to pretend parties.
- Students can make sales posters.
- Students can write a list of items to buy for their party.

Matching
- Have the children match various cards to the correct size of envelopes.
- Playing Old Maid and Go Fish with the cards in the center will help students match cards. The cards can also be used to play memory games.

Counting
- Birthday candles offer numerous opportunities for the children to count and sort different amounts.
- Paper cups, plates, and napkins can also be sold individually and counted for inventory.

Sorting
- The candles can be sorted by color into groups.
- All items will be sorted as they are restocked in the store.

Using a calendar and writing dates and time
- Encourage students to use the classroom calendar as they prepare their party invitations. Talk about what days and times would be best to schedule the party.

Adding money and making change
- Mark the various items with their cost, according to the grade level and ability of the children. Children can record the cost of the items chosen for purchase, add the cost, and give the store clerk the money to cover the cost. The clerk can figure out the change. A calculator can be used for the children to check their math.

Computer skills
- Children can visit a website that creates e-cards and send them to their parents or friends.
- Students can use a graphics program on the computer to print cards for the center.
- Children can find old-fashioned party games on the computer. They can read the directions and then teach the class how to play the game.

Other Ideas
- Have catalogues with party items (e.g., Oriental Trading Company) available and let the children use copies of the order sheet to prepare an order for the store. This task will involve reading, writing, and math.

- Talk about the jobs involved with this type of store. An additional job would be that of party planner. Ask the students what type of information a planner would need to know before being able to plan a party (e.g., age, number of guests).
- Using standard decks of cards, teach the children how to play games such as memory, solitaire, and War.

Book Connections

- Child, L. (2011). *This is actually my party*. New York, NY: Puffin.
- Hargreaves, R. (2007). *Mr. Birthday*. New York, NY: Price Stern Sloan.
- Kirk, D. (2007). *Miss Spider's tea party*. New York, NY: Scholastic.
- Numeroff, L. (2005). *If you give a pig a party*. New York, NY: HarperCollins.
- Otten, J. (2002). *Watch me make a birthday card*. New York, NY: Children's Press.

Items That Families Might Donate or Loan to the Center

- used cards (cut the front of the card off and glue it to a sheet of white cardstock to make it blank inside)
- old decks of playing cards, even ones with cards missing
- multioccasion cards
- leftover party favors or other party supplies

BED AND BATH SHOP CENTER

The bed and bath shop center is always enjoyable, in part because your classroom will smell clean the whole time and because the box taps into your teacher creativity with its overall simplicity and intended beauty. The intent of the box decoration is to make it look like a fancy bridal gift by gluing lace, decorative edging, white rick-rack, sequins, and beads on it. Affix decorations to the box lid as well. Superglue is the best choice for ensuring box longevity, but you can also spray clear enamel on it after the glue is dry to make it more durable. Or you can wrap the box with wedding wrapping paper, cover it in clear contact paper, and add a fancy bow or flowers. Place the box near the home living center, as this center is aligned with many of the home learning center's activities.

Many of the items you need for the bed and bath shop study should be brought from home or borrowed from your children's families. You also can store a few towels and washcloths and kitchen linens if they are not essential for use in your home. White sales are popular in January, so you might be able to find some inexpensive items that you can put into your box. Think about going to garage sales to pick up soap dishes, toothbrush holders, pillows, placemats, and other items to enhance center activity. A collection of hotel soaps will help with the sachet art project.

Contents

- towels, washcloths, and kitchen linens
- soap dishes, toothbrush holders, and other bathroom accessories
- pillows
- placemats, napkin rings, and kitchen accessories
- soaps

Content Information

- Explain to students what bed and bath shops are, and tell them that people buy all types of products for the home when they visit these specialty stores.
- Tell them that brides and grooms often visit bed and bath shops when they are planning to marry to prepare a list of gifts they need for their homes. Describe what a gift registry is and how it helps the couple's family and friends find wedding gifts.
- Help children understand that bed and bath shops are also good places to visit if someone wants to purchase a gift for someone who is moving into a new home.

BED AND BATH SHOP CENTER

Vocabulary Enrichment

- bath accessories
- scrubbers
- fragrances
- scents
- bath beads and bath gels
- soap bubbles
- suds
- decorator soaps
- soap dish
- toothbrush holder
- bleach
- sachet
- white sale
- mattress
- bunk beds
- bed sizes (twin, full, queen, king)
- futon
- feather pillow
- kitchen linens
- linen closet
- tablecloth
- bathmats
- shower curtain
- shower caddy
- gift registry
- candleholder
- curtain
- specialty store
- housewarming

Dramatic Play/Cooperation

- Placing a small plastic tub, soap, washcloths, and towels in the center will encourage students to bathe the classroom dolls using the linens. If you have sheets that fit a doll bed, have children make the bed. Demonstrate how to tuck in the corners of sheets. You can also add a soap dish and toothbrush holder to the center during this study.
- Add various decorator pillows to the home living center. Include feather pillows if you can find them (or a family might loan one to the classroom).
- A bottle of window cleanser and clean cloths will allow students to wash the mirror in the home living center and classroom windows if they choose.

Skills

Counting

- Place containers of bath beads in the center for children to count. Show children who can count to 100 or more how to count the beads by twos and fives. Talk to gifted children about what tens and ones mean with two-digit numbers (e.g., 2 tens and 5 ones equal 25).

Estimating

- Ask students to estimate how many beads are in each jar of bath beads. After they have written down their estimate, they should count to find out the actual number of beads. For the counting and estimating skills, you can substitute containers of cotton balls.

BED AND BATH SHOP CENTER

BED AND BATH SHOP CENTER

Understanding space and mass

- Count the same number of bath beads into each of two containers, one jar and one flat dish. Ask students to decide which one appears to be more. Then ask them to count the number of beads in each container to discover that the mass of objects will appear larger or smaller depending on the space they use.

Discriminating scents (odors)

- Put several unwrapped bars of soap in the center for children to smell and decide which they like best. Keep a tally of each child's selection so that a report can be made about the results of the smell test.

Rhyming words

- Second graders will enjoy a verbal game called ink pinks. Children give clues to two one-syllable words that rhyme for their peers to guess. Samples:
  - A colored sleeping place *(red bed)*
  - A lariat cleaner *(rope soap)*
  - Counting while in the tub *(bath math)*

- Two-syllable rhyming words are called inky pinkies. More samples:
  - Happy towel cloth *(merry terry)*
  - Washing strength *(shower power)*
  - Wetter dirty clothes container *(damper hamper)*

Fine-motor development

- Place a lock seam curtain rod and a curtain in the center so students can practice threading the rod through the runner at the top of the curtain. Use a shower curtain, shower curtain hooks, and a shower curtain rod for a similar experience.

Scientific investigation

- Put a small amount of bleach in a small dish and place it in the bed and bath shop center (this activity must be strictly supervised and you need to provide aprons from the art center or large shirts to cover children's clothing and goggles for eye protection). Allow children to experiment with various fabrics so they can observe how the chemical removes color from objects. Ask if they like the clean smell of bleach. Help students understand the toxic nature of bleach while carefully supervising the experience.

Writing

- Children can use a large piece of paper to write a list of items they want to place in a gift registry. Younger students may need to draw or cut out pictures of their gift requests from magazines and glue to the paper. Older students can write their selections on the paper. Collect all of the sheets to put into book form for your class gift registry.

Other Ideas

- Instructional recipes and the supplies necessary for making soap and bubbles can be located online, and you may want to consider this activity for your classroom. Making soap, however, has some risks, and you will need to supervise closely (or have a family member volunteer to assist). You can purchase glycerin at your local drugstore to enhance the bubble-blowing experience that children enjoy so much.
- Add bath toys to your water table. Ask students which ones are their favorites.
- Some students will delight in making soap sachets to take home. Show them how to cut soap shavings with scissors, butter knives, or cheese spreaders. Then provide squares or circles of net and ribbon for them to make the sachet. Place soap shavings in the middle of the net, bunch it up, and tie a ribbon around the tassel of net. Younger children will need assistance when it is time to tie the ribbon, and most children will need supervision with this experience.
- Provide wire clothes hangers in the art center for children to decorate. Show them how to curl gift-wrap ribbon and make construction paper spiral circles to attach to the hanger. You can also tie yarn and small pinecones to the hanger. Display these from the ceiling of your classroom if you can.
- Develop an environmental print album using toothpaste containers and soap wrappers. Position these in plastic photograph sheets for children to read as they look through the album. As a follow-up activity, you can ask children to tell which toothpaste they use or which soap is their favorite for graphing experiences.
- Share Hans Christian Andersen's story, *The Princess and the Pea*. Children may want to test the story's premise that only a princess can feel the pea through numerous layers of mattresses. Just for fun, bring in quilts, blankets, afghans, and a pea to stack in the classroom near the bed and bath shop center.
- Some children will choose to make washcloth pillows. Provide large needles, thread, and two washcloths per pillow and show children how to sew the cloths together, leaving an opening so that stuffing can be put inside. When the pillows are stuffed, the opening is sewn together. Stuffing is available at most craft or fabric stores.

Book Connections

- Boynton, S. (2007). *Bath time!* New York, NY: Workman.
- Mayer, M. (2001). *Just go to bed.* New York, NY: Random House.

BED AND BATH SHOP CENTER

Items That Families Might Donate or Loan to the Center

- linens, pillows, and other home bed and bath items
- unopened packages of sheets and pillowcases (to help children understand how these items are sold; they should be marked for easy return to the families who loan them)
- empty toothpaste boxes and soap wrappers

- kitchen linens, tablecloths, placemats, curtains, floor mats, shower curtains, shower hooks, and any other home accessories
- two washcloths from each family (optional; for the pillow making activity)
- hotel soaps
- outdated copies of most women's magazines

FLORIST CENTER

This center will most probably contain entirely new information for your students, as it is unlikely that they will have direct knowledge about florists. However, most children will enjoy playing in this center.

Decorating the florist center box is not absolutely necessary, because children's use of its contents is the main reason for having the container. However, if you want to decorate the box, you can draw or paint pictures of flowers all over it and cover it with clear contact paper. Another option is to request that children cut out flowers from magazines or seed catalogues and glue them onto the box. Giving older children the task of drawing flowers on the box will give them a sense of accomplishment. Again, covering the box with contact paper gives it some protection from year to year.

Contents

- an assortment of vases and flower pots
- florist's clay
- wire forms
- tissue paper
- ribbons

- plastic flowers and greenery
- decorator stakes or bamboo sticks
- packets of floral seeds
- flower seed catalogues
- a shadow box

Content Information

- Use a K-W-L strategy to learn what your students know about florists and florist shops. Ask children to tell what they know (K), and write their responses on a chart or chalkboard. Then ask them to tell you what they want to know (W) and write down the responses. When the study is over, talk to your children about what they have learned (L). When you chart these responses, students will recognize the knowledge they have acquired about florists.
- Discuss the children's favorite flowers. Talk to them about the reasons people purchase flowers for people they know and love (e.g., birthdays, new babies, Mother's Day).
- Share the familiar phrase "April showers bring May flowers" and ask students to define its meaning. Clarify their responses as needed.
- Ask children if they would like to prepare a flower garden. Approach your director or principal about locating a spot on the playground for your classroom garden or create a container garden near a classroom window.

Vocabulary Enrichment

- florist
- florist shop
- floral arrangement (fresh and dried)
- flower garden
- greenery/filler
- florist's clay
- types of flowers (e.g., roses, carnations, daisies, other flowers popular in your region)
- fern
- moss
- wire forms

Dramatic Play/Cooperation

- Some children pick dandelions, bitter weeds, or other wild flowers that sprout up on the playground during April or May, so this natural experience will serve as a springboard to the florist study.

Skills

Rhyming riddles

- Develop riddles based on the vocabulary for students to guess. Begin each by telling what word will rhyme with the answer. For example, tell children that the answer will rhyme with *rose*. Ask them to name a part of a person's face (answer: *nose*).

Repeated addition/multiplication

- Make several identical sets of index cards with flower stickers so students can practice addition. If a set of six cards has five rose stickers on each card, students can count (or add) to determine that the total number of roses is 30. With practice, children should be able to tell that six (cards) times five (roses) is 30. Name this process as multiplication. Challenge students by preparing more difficult mathematical sets.

Writing stories

- First and second graders should be able to write a story about what florists do.

Forming plural words

- Give children a list of flower names and ask them to form plurals. Remember to use various plural forms (*-s, -es, -ies*) with words such as *roses, irises, daisies,* and *lilies.*

Measuring

- Provide flowers with different lengths of stems. Have the children measure them using a ruler and place them into vases that are marked with the different lengths. You can make it challenging by having stems that are 1/2" difference in length.

Reading
- Prepare cards with written descriptions of flowers on them, then ask students to read the description and find the flowers to fill the order (e.g., two purple flowers with stems that are 8" long). To make it more challenging, provide the scientific name so that they will have to go to a flower identification book and look up what that flower looks like to fill the order.

Other Ideas
- Work with groups of children to develop an alphabetic listing of flowers. Encourage your students to talk with their families to find examples of flowers for difficult letters such as *q* and *x*. The Internet can provide answers for letters that challenge children.
- Place flowers (real or plastic) on a table in the classroom with pots, florist's clay, and wire forms. Encourage students to form flower arrangements for display. *Note:* Plastic flowers and greenery go on sale in January as hobby shops and garden centers prepare for incoming spring inventory. This is the best time to purchase items for your florist center.
- If your students choose to plant a garden, photograph their efforts to prepare the soil, plant the seeds, water the plants, and eventually pick the flowers. Make a classroom display on a mural or in an album to share with their families or visitors to their classroom. This collection of photographs will help students understand the natural growth of plants, especially if some thrive and others do not.
- Ask small groups of children to draw posters that show the various parts of plants (e.g., roots, stems, leaves, flowers). They may need to look this information up online.
- Show students a shadow box and tell them that they can make one, too. Put all sorts of materials in the art center for them to use (e.g., plastic flowers, fern, moss, twigs, dried leaves, acorns, sweet gum balls, small pebbles, and other items). They should glue their selections to the inside of a shoebox and the creation should dry thoroughly. The teacher (or classroom volunteer) should cut a hole in the box lid for each child. For a more professional look, cellophane can be taped inside the lid, so that it will look like a glass pane. Superglue the lid onto the box, and let students take their creations home as a keepsake. If this study is used in May, the shadow box can become a Mother's Day gift.
- Ask students to think of flower names that people use for their children's names (e.g., Lily, Daisy, Pansy, Rose, Dahlia). They can ask their families to help generate names. Continue collecting names for as long as the florist study continues.

- Prepare and bring a terrarium to the classroom so students can see cacti in sand. Talk about climates that affect plant growth such as the dry, arid soil that some plants prefer.
- Some flowers (roses and pansies are good selections) will make faint marks on paper when they are used as if they were crayons or markers. The light tints produce pleasing results for children's artwork.

Book Connections

- Azarian, M. (2000). *A gardener's alphabet*. Boston, MA: Houghton Mifflin.
- Bogacki, T. (2000). *My first garden*. New York, NY: Farrar, Straus and Giroux.
- Ehlert, L. (1992). *Planting a rainbow*. New York, NY: Sandpiper.
- Glaser, O. (2000). *Round the garden*. New York, NY: Abrams.

Items That Families Might Donate or Loan to the Center

- shoe boxes
- flowers from their gardens or plastic flowers for the floral arranging experience
- decorative pots, fern, decorative stakes, bamboo, cattails, or moss
- terrarium

FLORIST CENTER

HAIR SALON CENTER

When making this center, be sure that the children understand that there is to be no real hair cutting. Having scissors that don't actually cut may be helpful, but this still needs to be stressed so that children don't use other scissors from the classroom.

In a hair salon, supplies that are used by the stylists are often stored in plain sight on shelves for easy access. This box will be the supply area for the salon. Use the one open side cut (see Figure 2): On one of the long sides at both corners, you will need to cut down from the top edge to the bottom, freeing this side. Fold the long side out and lay it flat on the table. If the teacher wants to make the storage area a little more complex, a shelf can be made to further divide up the space by taking corrugated cardboard from another box. A piece should be cut that will fit lengthwise inside the box, but with an additional 6 inches added to the piece. Fold this piece so that there are 3 inches on each side, making an elongated U. Place the U upside down inside the storage area. Bins or tubs can now be used under the shelf and bottles can be placed on top of the shelf. The outside of the box can be decorated with words for objects found in salons. The box is now ready for the hair care items to be positioned in it.

Contents

- small samples of shampoo and conditioner (full ones if children are washing a doll's hair)
- various hair products
- scissors that *won't* cut hair
- a wrap to place around the client
- apron for the hair washer to wear
- mirrors
- bins for storage
- curlers
- electric tools, such a blow dryer or hair trimmers (should have their cords cut off)
- various length combs and special types of brushes

Content Information

- The amount of prior knowledge that the children have will depend upon whether or not they have their hair cut in a salon or go with their parents when they have their hair cut.
- Have a class discussion about what happens when you go to get your hair cut and all of the steps involved.
- Use the different items from the center and explain what those items are and why they are used in a hair salon.

HAIR SALON CENTER

HAIR SALON CENTER

Vocabulary Enrichment

- hair stylist
- unisex
- reservation
- permanent
- highlights
- styling
- walk ins
- manicure
- pedicure
- trends
- hair dryer
- flat iron
- makeover
- shampoo
- conditioner
- hair spray
- curling iron
- coloring
- waves
- curls
- haircuts

Dramatic Play/Cooperation

- If you are going to allow the children to use small bottles of shampoo to wash a doll's hair, you will need to place the center near a sink. If no real washing of hair will be done, children may still pretend to wash hair by using empty bottles and a homemade sink.
- Have a telephone available for the students to make appointments.
- Students can use wigs and hair extensions in their dramatic play.

Skills

Matching

- Using bottles of nail polish and lipstick, have students match the colors of nail polish to the same color of lipstick. This idea came from Peggy Hutson, a kindergarten teacher. She took bottles of half used nail polish and old tubes of lipstick, removed all of the lipstick and cut a dowel rod (obtained at a home supply store) to fit into the now empty tube. Then she used each of the nail polishes to paint a corresponding dowel and glued it into the empty lipstick container. After gluing the bottles of nail polish shut, she put them in her center for a matching activity.

Name writing

- Have students write their name in the appointment book when they arrive at the salon.

Counting

- Use the curlers and have boxes or tubs labeled with numerals. The children will count the correct number of curlers into each. Be sure to have numbers that are high enough to challenge all of the children.

Sorting
- Have the children sort curlers by color, size, or type.
- Sort boxes of hair coloring by color, number on the box, or type.

Measuring
- Use a ruler to measure various sizes of combs. Record their length in both inches and in centimeters.
- Use a ruler to measure different lengths of hairpieces or hair extensions.

Making and reading charts
- Students can make a chart or poster to hang in the center that shows the steps for getting a haircut at a salon.
- Students can make a chart to show the different hair colors found in the class.

Create artwork
- Let the children dip some of the sponge curlers in a shallow pan of paint and roll the roller part across paper to make a design. Curlers that are self-hooking are the best to use. The part that closes on the curler can be used as the handle when painting.

Other Ideas
- Invite a hair stylist to your classroom and ask her to bring her styling tools, pictures, and wigs to share with the children.
- Do comparison studies on brands of shampoo as to which one makes the most suds and keeps its suds the longest.
- Test the difference between permanent hair dyes and wash-in hair dyes. Check with a local hair salon to see if you can get samples of hair for your tests. This activity should be supervised.
- Use a thermometer to measure how hot a hair dryer gets.
- Have hair styling magazines available for students to read or look at in the reading center.

Book Connections
- Ehrlich, F. (2003). *Does a yak get a haircut?* Maplewood, NJ: Blue Apple.
- Marek, C. (2005). *Sara's 1st hair cut.* Canton, MI: Zoe Life Publishing.
- Wilhelm, H. (1998). *Don't cut my hair!* New York, NY: Scholastic.

HAIR SALON CENTER

HAIR SALON CENTER

Items That Families Might Donate or Loan to the Center

- all types and sizes of curlers (e.g., electric curlers, sponge curlers, curlers used with permanents)
- dolls with hair (for use with the curlers and hair washing experiences)
- empty bottles of hair products
- small shampoo and conditioner bottles from hotels
- old curling irons and dryers with the power cords removed
- hairpieces, wigs, hair extensions (can be used for before and after the trip to the hair salon)
- empty hair dye boxes

SPORTS STORE CENTER

The sports store center box and its development depend on your understanding of the sports interests in your community. Some areas of the country focus on specific sports (e.g., basketball in Indiana, football in Texas). Conducting an environmental scan to determine the most popular sports in your area should provide insight about your box decorations.

Take into consideration your children's interests, too. Many young children attend sporting events when their older siblings are involved. Representing popular high school or middle school teams might be a plan of action. Using your school colors and putting local mascot decals on the box are good design features. Or you may decorate each side of the box with pictures of balls and equipment that represent different sports.

Placing the sports center box near the cabinet or closet that stores your outdoor play equipment indicates the flexibility of the sports store topic. Dramatic play may occur outdoors, although many activities can be implemented indoors.

Contents

- sweatband and wristbands
- bobble-head sports figure dolls
- sports schedules
- photographs of ballparks, stadiums, and teams
- sports hats and caps
- child-sized helmets
- knee pads
- balls (baseball, softball, tennis balls, golf balls, ping pong balls, football, basketball, soccer ball)
- samples of tickets and scorecards
- sports decals
- pom-poms
- a CD or audio file of "Take Me Out to the Ballgame"
- baseball cards
- sports jerseys
- posters of familiar players
- child-sized golf clubs
- bowling pins
- sports drinks
- a catcher's mitt
- cash register
- table

Content Information

- Talk to students about sports, asking them to tell about their favorite sports. Talk about the training and health regimen athletes follow in order to excel in their sport.
- Differentiate between individual and team sports. Some sports (e.g., ice skating, long distance running, long jumping) are usually considered to be individual sports, but can become team sports if athletes participate in relays.

SPORTS STORE CENTER

- Help children understand that athletes have positive attitudes about winning and losing. Sports figures know that it is impossible to win all of the time, and they are prepared to deal with failure when it comes.
- Talk about the roles of the coach and trainer for athletes and how they want to help young players become better in their chosen sports.
- Discuss the warm-up time athletes participate in when they prepare for sports. Show students how to stretch to maximize their muscle flexibility and perseverance.
- Tell students that scorekeepers record statistics for athletes and their performances during sporting events. This information is shared with sports announcers and sportswriters to help the public understand how well the players and teams are doing. Explain that numbers on uniforms allow scorekeepers to track team and individual performance.
- Talk to children about team spirit and teach them a cheer they will recognize if they attend local sporting events.
- Help students understand the difference between amateur and professional sports. Discuss the need for sportsmanlike conduct when players participate in athletic events. Tell students that teams and players are penalized or fined when they fail to exhibit appropriate behavior during games and competitions.
- If you are using this center in the springtime, talk about the sports season that is winding down (basketball) and the sports season that is beginning (baseball). Explain that most sports have seasonal cycles, allowing athletes to train for sports.

Vocabulary Enrichment

- athlete
- coach
- trainer
- team
- equipment
- protective gear
- knee pads
- shoulder pads
- training
- muscles
- stamina
- perseverance
- referee
- umpire

- sportsmanlike conduct
- kick
- throw
- catch
- swing
- sports injury
- bandages
- gym
- swimming pool
- Olympics (summer and winter)
- Olympic sports
- fishing equipment
- team spirit
- cheerleaders

- scores
- scorekeeper
- whistle
- time
- timekeeper
- penalty
- ballpark
- stadium

- track
- track and field events
- mascot
- statistics
- sports announcer
- sportswriters
- sports legend

Dramatic Play/Cooperation

- Bring in an inflatable pool (or use the one stored in the amusement park box), positioning it near the sports center box. Add oars so children can pretend to row a boat. If you add child-sized fishing poles, children can pretend to fish from the boat.
- Bowling pins and a ball suitable for the classroom allow students to bowl.
- A duffel bag might also encourage sports play if you also have jerseys and sports equipment available to put into it.
- Children can roll tennis and ping pong balls to one another if they sit in a circle on the floor. If you have a few pompoms handy, children can pretend to be cheerleaders.

Skills

Kicking, throwing, and catching

- Ask volunteers to come in during the sports center study to practice skills with individual children.

Word searches

- Find smaller words within larger words (e.g., baseball, basketball, protective gear, season schedules) by rearranging letters. Children can keep a listing of these to determine how many they write for each larger word.

Writing

- Ask your students to adopt a favorite home team and interview members of the team to write reports. Help students develop a consistent interview form with questions about the following topics:
  - o what they like about the specific sport they play;
  - o what skills are needed for playing the sport;
  - o what is easiest and most difficult about their performance during games;
  - o memorable game experiences they recall; and
  - o their plans for continuing to play the sport in the future.

SPORTS STORE CENTER

Compile these reports into a "Favorite Home Team Book" for the entire class and family members to read.

Statistics

- A few students will be interested in checking statistical information for their favorite players. Professional organizations (e.g., National Basketball Association) report statistics for their players, and children can find this information by going online. Tell children about some of the information they can learn about their heroes such as:
  o how many points players have made during their careers;
  o the number of passes quarterbacks have completed;
  o how many tournaments golfers and bowlers have won;
  o the number of matches tennis players have played and won;
  o how many homeruns baseball players have hit and runs they have batted in; and
  o the number of Olympic awards individuals have received.

Point out to children that team statistics are also available for their favorite teams.

- Very advanced children can be challenged to figure out the statistics for pretend players. Provide the children with the numbers they need and allow them to use a calculator to do the computations.

Other Ideas

- Have a sports drink for snack one day. Talk about the benefits sports drinks have to boost energy for a short period of time.
- You might want to set up an obstacle course to practice sports skills during this study. You can add opportunities to run, hop, jump, skip, and stretch to the obstacle course.
- Plan a favorite team day, asking students to wear clothing representing their favorite sports franchise. Have a selection of decals available to pin on shirts or extra (donated) clothing for this special celebration for those children who cannot afford sports clothes or forget to wear them.
- Show students how to sit back to back on the floor and join their arms at their elbows. They can row back and forth as they sing "Row, Row, Row Your Boat."
- Begin a sports legend display on a bulletin board in your classroom. Suggested sports figures to post on this board are Dirk Nowitzki and Tina Thompson (basketball), Albert Pujols and Sammy Sosa (baseball), Phil Mickelson and Annika Sorenstam (golf), Roger Federer or the Williams sisters (tennis), the

Lopez family (taekwondo Olympic competitors), Melissa Gregory and Denis Petukhov (ice skating), and other legends that are their favorites.

Book Connections

- Bildner, P. (2006). *Shoeless Joe and black Betsy.* New York, NY: Simon & Schuster.
- Prelutsky, J. (2011). *Good sports.* New York, NY: Dragonfly.

Items That Families Might Donate or Loan to the Center

- sports equipment (have names on it so it can be returned easily)
- volunteer time to assist with sports skill-building activities

SPORTS STORE CENTER

PAINT AND HARDWARE STORE CENTER

As is true in several other centers in this section, children's understanding of resources in their community will influence the development of this specific box. Plan the box around the type of store children may have visited, whether it is a national franchise or a locally owned business. Most paint and hardware stores focus on the supplies that carpenters and builders need, while others appeal to a broader customer base. You are likely to find decorative home items, garden supplies, paint, wallpaper selections, and products that any do-it-yourself homeowner might desire. Enjoy the process of making choices for your box, but be prepared to add materials that children suggest as their dramatic play emerges.

The exterior decoration of the center box may be as simple as cutting out a local store's logo to place on the side of the box and putting contact paper over it for protection. You might also consider letting your children decorate the box. If you include several packages of popsicle sticks inside the box, some children will spend their time gluing these onto the sides of the box as part of their dramatic play of building. Following this practice means that you will need to replace the box and the popsicle sticks annually, but the perseverance and fine-motor skills required to accomplish this task is specifically important for young children. Also consider having more than one box available to decorate if children are attracted to this activity.

Contents

- hammer
- screwdriver
- mallet
- tape measure
- ruler
- yardstick
- twine
- popsicle sticks
- screws
- nuts and bolts
- washers
- nails
- paintbrushes
- paint sticks
- short lengths of chain and rope
- at least one pair of work gloves
- small pieces of wood (various sizes)
- Styrofoam pieces
- a square piece of door screen
- door knobs
- drawer pulls
- paint chips
- wallpaper and carpet samples
- photographs of local paint and hardware stores (store them in freezer bags or envelopes)
- photographs of carpenters and construction workers doing their jobs
- sample home blueprints
- goggles for eye protection
- sandpaper
- magnets

Content Information

- Ask children if their families have ever been involved in a home remodeling or building project. Give them an opportunity to talk about how they have helped with these projects. Talk to children about all of the products they can purchase when they go to a paint and hardware store.
- Discuss what carpenters, builders, and construction workers do in their jobs. Show photographs of these individuals doing their work if you have them. If it is available, show an apron a person wears that holds tools and nails he or she needs for building.
- Talk to older students about the six types of simple machines (inclined plane, wedge, screw, lever, pulley, and wheel and axle). Help students think of examples for each and show samples if they are available. Talk about how machines help construction workers and carpenters when they work.

Vocabulary Enrichment

- blueprints
- home repair
- remodeling
- building
- ladder
- sawhorse
- hammer
- mallet
- saw
- screw
- screwdriver
- lever
- pulley
- wheel
- axle
- frame
- window frame
- walls
- ceiling
- cabinets
- flooring
- wallpaper
- plumbing
- fixtures
- lighting
- goggles
- concrete
- cement
- drop cloth

Dramatic Play/Cooperation

- Placing the paint and hardware store in the block center should facilitate dramatic play. If you can locate a sawhorse or two to include in the center (or if a family can loan one to your classroom), the play will seem more authentic. This activity will need to be supervised, especially if you are going to allow children to hammer nails into Styrofoam pieces or lumber. Demonstrate how to hold nails to avoid accidents.

PAINT AND HARDWARE STORE CENTER

113

- As children pretend, they need to wear goggles to show their understanding that workers wear them to protect their eyes.
- Place large pieces of paper, rulers, and blue map pencils in the center so children can design their own blueprints. Have professional blueprints available for children to use to guide them.

Skills

Tracing

- Encourage children to trace various items onto paper (washers, hammers, or mallets). Display their work in the classroom.
- Children can trace items onto graph paper and compare the areas of two different items by counting the squares that each one covers. They will also have to figure in partial squares.

Measuring

- Use nonstandard measures and ask children to measure pieces of rope or chain. Some stores mark measurements on the floor, so employees do not have to search for the tape measure each time it is needed. Older children can use rulers and yardsticks for measurement purposes. Talk to children about the need for accurate measurements when people build or do home remodeling.
- With small pieces of real wood of differing widths (2" x 4", 1" x 2", 1" x 4"), have the children record the actual measurements. A lot of wood marked with a specific size is not actually that size. Have them figure out the difference.

Sorting

- Place nuts and bolts into a box and ask children to sort them into a plastic divided tray.
- More advanced students can sort wire that is different diameters in width. They can use a template that is marked in 1/8" increments to help them.

Matching

- Challenge children to match nuts and bolts and screw each bolt into its accompanying part. A similar matching activity can be used with locks and keys.
- Provide various wallpaper designs with their corresponding paint chip color (or plain wallpaper) and ask children to match them.

Drawing and critical thinking

- After looking at sample blueprints, let the children draw plans for a room in their house or a playhouse. Have a checklist of questions for them to use to evaluate their drawings (e.g., Does your door open in or out? Are electrical outlets marked on your plans?).

- There are some simple design websites for teachers to use when setting up their classrooms. Have the children use one of these websites to draw their classroom and add the furniture that is in the classroom.

Other Ideas

- Dip washers, decorative doorknobs and drawer pulls, pieces of carpet, and pieces of rope or chain in tempera paint to make interesting designs on paper.
- Children can also glue pieces of rope, odd pieces of carpet, sandpaper, and scrap pieces of lumber onto poster board to make carpenter collages.
- Using a square piece of door screen and a paintbrush (or an old toothbrush), spatter tempera paint onto large pieces of manila paper.
- Paint a piece of classroom furniture by placing it on a painter's drop cloth in the art center and using water (instead of paint). Paint the sidewalk on the playground with paintbrushes and water that has been colored with food dyes. Rain will wash away the color when the weather changes.
- Provide a painted board for students to remove the paint with sandpaper. Give them the knowledge that removing paint is a time-consuming process.
- Place magnets, magnetic filings, and numerous small objects magnets will attract on a table near the center, allowing students to explore the properties of magnets.
- First and second graders can learn about compound words. The words *hardware, sandpaper, wallpaper, paintbrush, sawhorse,* and *sidewalk* are just a few words that can be used with this theme to help children understand how words are put together to form compounds. Begin a list on a large chart or add words to the classroom word wall.

Book Connections

- Barton, B. (1981). *Building a house.* New York, NY: Greenwillow.

Items That Families Might Donate or Loan to the Center

- empty toolboxes
- empty, clean paint cans
- paint sticks
- unused wallpaper or border pieces

- sawhorse
- wire
- small lengths of rope or chain
- locks and keys
- scrap pieces of lumber or carpet

PAINT AND HARDWARE STORE CENTER

TRAVEL AGENCY CENTER

This center will expose children to different places in the world. Although more and more people use the Internet for their travel needs, there are still travel agencies in most cities. Visiting them and asking when new brochures arrive will help you in planning for this center, assuming that the agencies will give you outdated brochures.

For this center, you can use most of the items that you have in your office center. The box can just be used for storage of the travel agency items that will be specific to this center. You will need some type of display for travel brochures that you acquire. An easy way to display the brochures would be to buy dollar store napkin holders and line them up along a shelf or window ledge. Other options would be buying cardboard brochure holders or using plastic stacking desk trays. The classroom computer can be used and bookmarks can be created for different online travel agencies. Cruise lines, airlines, and trains all have sites that the children could explore.

Pick up colorful brochures at state and city welcome centers or tourist offices. If you plan ahead, you can gather many brochures from places that you travel. Each U.S. state will send you a road map and guide to things to do in the state if you contact its tourism office. A map of your state or the U.S. can be displayed on the wall behind your center. Be sure and hang it low enough that the children can look at the map. They will enjoy trying to find places that they know.

The center will need a telephone, but you will also need another phone (placed close by) for students to call and order airline tickets, check on reservations, and ask for information. A file box with folders can be used to place information on cruises, places to visit, and attractions.

Contents

- office supplies from the office center
- toy telephone
- filing box with file folders
- brochures, folders, and some way to display them
- maps (U.S. map, your state road map, and a world map)

Content Information

- People can have a travel agency make the arrangements for trips they want to take.
- The travel agent can make arrangements for airfare, hotels, cruises, train trips, car rentals, or other needs.
- Your itinerary tells you what you will be doing on what days. It is your schedule.

- Travel agencies have color brochures from many places that show pictures and tell details of trips it is possible to take.

Vocabulary Enrichment

- excursion (shore excursion, land excursion)
- booking
- gratuity
- tours
- escorted tour
- package deals
- agent
- discount
- commission
- timetables
- reservations

- passport
- tourist trap
- tourist attraction
- bed and breakfast (B & B)
- resort
- roadside attraction
- rail
- travel agent
- tour guide
- destination
- itinerary
- accommodations

Dramatic Play/Cooperation

- Set up your travel agency using the items from the office center. Add the brochures, tape the maps to the wall, and place the telephone in a prominent place on a table in the center.
- Role-play with the students by calling the travel agency center and telling the agent that you would like to go on a cruise. Ask what brochures are available for you to look at. The agent will tell you a place or two and invite you to come into the agency to look at the brochures.
- Continue the role-play with you as the agent and another child as the customer. This will allow the children to understand some of the services that travel agents can provide.

Skills

Learning personal information
- Give students a card from the Rolodex and have them practice writing their name and phone number on the card.

Alphabetical order
- Let the children put the cards from the activity above in the Rolodex, thereby practicing learning the order of the alphabet.
- Using the filing system, have students place the brochures in alphabetical order.

TRAVEL AGENCY CENTER

Reading schedules or charts

- Go online, and find and print a schedule for buses and trains. Have cards with little scenarios written on them that will require the children to read the schedule and do some problem solving. For example, "Jimmy needs to be at Lamar Station no later than 2 p.m. Which train must he take in order to get there on time?"

Adding with regrouping

- Have students put together package deals for airfares and accommodations. Give them price lists for three different airlines and hotels. They have to add the prices to see which package is the best deal. You can also add in car rentals for a more challenging activity.

Planning healthy meals

- Bring in food sale ads and have the children plan a healthy breakfast for their B & B using items that are on sale. They should add the prices to determine how much money they will need to take to the store. They can check their answer with the calculator.

Writing and using technology

- Using the world map, have the children choose a place that they would like to visit. They can go online once they pick out a place, type in "tourism," and get ideas of what is available. Students can then write a promotional piece for the classroom newsletter and make a brochure about this place.

Locating places on maps and globes

- Give students a list of places to find on a map or globe. If you laminate the list, they can use a dry-erase marker to check them off as they find them.
- Give them riddles to solve by finding places on the map. For example, "I am a big city at the mouth of the Mississippi River. I am _____."

Other Ideas

- Go online to one of the cruise line websites. Pictures of ships and the various decks are available for you to show the children what large cruise ships look like inside. You can do the same thing with railway packages.
- Invite a travel agent to come to your class and talk to students about his responsibilities.
- Bring in cars from a toy train set and talk about the purpose of each car and which cars are for carrying people.
- Have a digital camera available for the children to take photos of each other for their "passports."
- Turn the home center into a B & B for dramatic play. Students can write out a menu for the breakfast that they will serve their customers.
- This is a good time to discuss water safety and sun protection.

- Use this time to talk about the cultures of different countries. Your agency might run a special on trips to Mexico. Bring in pictures of different areas of Mexico and foods that can be sampled, teach a few words of Spanish, and mention ways that Mexico is similar to and different from the U.S. Use a Venn diagram to show this visually.
- Teach the children to hula. Explain to them that the movements have meanings. You can find some easy movements to teach the children either online or in library books.

Book Connections

- Berenstain, S., & Berenstain, J. (2006). *The Berenstain Bears and too much car trip.* New York, NY: HarperCollins.
- Brown, M. (1995). *Arthur's family vacation: An Arthur adventure.* New York, NY: Little, Brown.
- Mayer, B. (2008). *All aboard! A traveling alphabet.* New York, NY: Margaret K. McElderry.
- Roberts, S. (2005). *We all go traveling by.* Cambridge, MA: Barefoot Books.

Items That Families Might Donate or Loan to the Center

- color posters that advertise places of interest for travel (especially if anyone in the family works for a travel agent, airline, cruise, bus, or train system)
- travel brochures or travel guides

TRAVEL AGENCY CENTER

Chapter 9   Food Theme Centers

Food centers also are very much a part of the experiences that young children have and share. Even children from poverty will have some experience with pizza, cookies, ice cream, and fast food drive-throughs. The centers chosen for this chapter reflect common interests and experiences of young children. Use these centers as a guide and develop other centers that will appeal to your particular group of children. Restaurants that are readily available in your community are always a good choice. Mexican, Chinese, or fried chicken restaurants are three that are present in most communities. Many restaurants and fast food restaurants will give you clean paper supplies that they use in their business. Some will even give you a copy of their menu and old prizes that they have left from previous children's meals. You just have to be willing to ask.

BAKERY CENTER

Most young children will be very familiar with a bakery, whether it is the one in the grocery store where they get a free cookie or the local donut shop. The salt dough food items that can be made for this center are appealing to all children. The items are so realistic looking that a visitor to our classroom thought we actually were allowing the children to play with real food.

The box for this center can be made to look like a stove or a counter in a bakery. Often, the teacher will decide how to use the box based on other materials already existing in the classroom. If there is already a stove, it might serve the class better to make the box resemble a counter where children place their orders and where the items are displayed.

If it is to be made into a stove, it will have four burners on the top and an oven door cut into the long side of the box. Cut the door so that about 3 inches of box remain between the door and the edge of the box. A cheap handle for the oven door may be purchased at a home supply store for under $2 and can be attached by screwing it through a tongue depressor or other strip of thin wood. For added support for the oven door, tack or glue a thin piece of wood, such as molding, on the inside edge of the box that is under the oven door. On the two sides of the stove, place self-sticking hooks for hanging utensils. After placing the utensils on the hooks, take a marker and trace around the outline of each.

On a cookie tray, make 12 circles the same size as the chocolate chip cookies made from the salt dough and number the circles from 1 to 12. Write the color words on self-sticking labels and stick them to empty berry containers. Divide the shirt box into three sections using a wide black marker. Label the sections with the words *sacks, forks,* and *napkins.*

Contents

- 18 salt dough sugar cookies in three colors (see salt dough recipe in Appendix C)
- 24 salt dough donut holes
- 12 salt dough donuts
- 12 salt dough chocolate chip cookies (with 1–12 chocolate chips colored on each cookie)
- 6 salt dough cupcakes in a cupcake pan
- 6 small, red, round salt dough cookies
- 6 small, yellow, triangular salt dough cookies
- 6 small, blue, rectangular salt dough cookies
- cookie sheets
- measuring spoons
- bowls
- spoons
- spatulas and scrapers
- tongs
- egg beater
- play money

- cash register
- 6 quart-size plastic strawberry containers
- several pint-size blackberry containers
- lunch sacks
- sticky notes

- pencils
- plastic spoons and forks
- paper napkins (or the school's paper towels cut into halves)
- chef hats or hair covering of some sort

Content Information

- A bakery offers many different types of baked products. They might have donuts, bagels, pastries, kolaches, muffins, cakes, and cookies.
- The baker is the person who does the cooking.
- When making baked goods, you have a recipe that tells you what ingredients to put in, how much of each ingredient, how long to bake it, and at what temperature it needs to be baked.

Vocabulary Enrichment

- spatula
- measuring cups
- measuring spoons
- teaspoon
- tablespoon
- dough
- knead
- muffin pan
- recipe
- tongs

- ingredients
- burner
- egg beater
- scrapers
- cookie sheet
- bagel
- pastry
- kolache
- croissant
- eclair

Dramatic Play/Cooperation

- Children may use the assortment of baking utensils, spoons, spatulas, cookie sheets and pans, measuring spoons, sacks, and play money to pretend to bake and sell the products in the bakery.
- The table from the home center or another small table can be used for sit-down dining.
- Have the children use play dough and design special cookies.
- Students can use the writing center to prepare sales posters and other ads for the store.

Skills

One-to-one correspondence
- As the students place the cupcakes in the cupcake pan, they will be practicing one-to-one correspondence.
- Placing cookies on outlines of circles on a cookie sheet is another way for the children to practice one-to-one correspondence.

Matching
- Using the outlines of the different utensils that have been drawn on the outside sides of the box, the children can match the utensil to the correct outline by hanging the utensils on the hook on the box.

Counting
- Using the chocolate chip cookies, students can count the chocolate chips in the cookies and place the cookie on the correct numeral on the cookie sheet.
- The children can also use the sticky notes and a marker to mark the blackberry containers with a numeral and then count the correct number of donut holes into the containers.
- Sacks can be numbered and students can count cookies into the sacks according to the numeral on the sack.
- Make some of the cookies have larger numbers of chocolate chips and mark another cookie sheet with the corresponding higher numbers, allowing for the needs of more advanced children. The children can count the chocolate chips in these cookies and place the cookie on the correct numeral on the cookie sheet.
- Students can also use the sticky notes to mark the strawberry containers with a higher numeral and then count the correct number of donut holes into the container.
- Students can practice counting very large numbers by counting piles of chocolate chips that have been made from salt dough, or you may spray paint some dried beans brown to represent the chocolate chips.

Patterns
- Using another cookie sheet and the small shape cookies, the children can extend patterns that the teacher begins or create their own patterns.

Sorting
- With the three different colors of sugar cookies, students can sort the sugar cookies into the quart containers according to the color of the cookies. They can also be given a mixture of cookies, donuts, and donut holes and can sort the items by type.

Initial consonant sounds and reading
- Have a box sectioned off with words marking where the various items in the center are to be placed. This will allow the children to use initial consonant

sounds as they place the forks, spoons, and napkins in the appropriate section of the box.

- Make cards that have orders to be filled. For example, 20 doughnut holes, five blue sugar cookies, and three yellow sugar cookies.

Color words
- Color words can also be learned as students place the sugar cookies in boxes that are marked with the color words of the sugar cookies.

Graphing
- Bring in several different types of cookies or baked goods. Have the children sample each one and construct a graph according to their favorite.

Other Ideas
- Take a field trip to a local bakery or, if this is not possible, check the Internet for a virtual field trip to a bakery.
- Use the Internet to find recipes that you can make in your classroom.
- Compare pita bread, tortillas, and sandwich bread. Discuss how they are different and how they are the same. Show the children how this can be placed on a Venn diagram.
- Expose the children to the different multicultural baked foods that are available in your area. Have a tasting party and then graph their preferences.
- Use store-bought sugar cookies and icing in tubes and let students decorate the cookies for a snack.
- Make bread in your classroom. A bread machine is an easy way to do this. Allow the children to measure the ingredients.
- Bring in dry yeast and talk about the function of yeast in bread making. Have a glass of cold water, warm water, hot water, and warm water with a quarter of a teaspoon of sugar dissolved in it. Have the children predict what they think will happen when you add two teaspoons of yeast to each one. Observe and record the results every 2 minutes.

Book Connections
- Hennessy, B. G. (1990). *Jake baked the cake.* New York, NY: Penguin.
- Morris, A. (1993). *Bread, bread, bread.* New York, NY: HarperCollins.
- Numeroff, L. J. (2010). *If you give a mouse a cookie* (25th anniversary ed.). New York, NY: HarperCollins.
- Numeroff, L. J. (1991). *If you give a moose a muffin.* New York, NY: HarperCollins.

BAKERY CENTER

Items That Families Might Donate or Loan to the Center

- kitchen utensils and pans (spatulas, cupcake pans, bowls, cookies sheets)
- plastic fruit containers from the grocery store
- napkins
- plastic forks and spoons

- measuring cups and spoons
- lunch-size sacks
- any special recipes for baked goods that they would be willing to bake, bring to school, and talk about the food and its history

BAKERY CENTER

ICE CREAM PARLOR CENTER

Most children love ice cream. For this center, you can turn this box into the ice cream freezer in the parlor. Cut a large door on the top of the box and affix a handle to the door. Containers for the ice cream can then be placed into the freezer, ready for serving.

A visit to a local ice cream parlor will give you more ideas. You can also take pictures to use with the children when talking about how orders are filled. You will need a holder for the ice cream cones. This can be made by cutting round holes in the top of a box that is shoebox size. Be sure that the cones fit down into the holes about halfway. Ice cream cones can be made by laminating brown paper and then forming a cone and taping the ends together. Ice cream can either be colored balls of Styrofoam, play dough, or cheap plastic balls.

Contents

- empty cartons for the different flavors of ice cream, along with signs identifying the flavor
- ice cream scoops
- small spoons
- single serving containers
- empty bottles of sauces and toppings
- toy cash register
- money
- purses and wallets
- order pads
- ice cream novelties (made from salt dough and then wrapped in wrappers)

Content Information

- There are many different types of items that people refer to as ice cream, and each of these types may come in many different flavors.
- Ice cream parlors often carry other items such as sundaes, ice cream sodas, milk shakes, banana splits, and ice cream cakes.

Vocabulary Enrichment

- frozen custard
- frozen yogurt
- sorbet
- gelato
- ice crystals
- flavorings
- waffle cone
- sugar cone
- scoops (as refer to the number)
- soft serve
- spigot
- freezer
- sherbet
- snow cones
- dry ice
- brain freeze
- ice cream novelties

Dramatic Play/Cooperation

- The table from the home center or another small table can become a table in the parlor.
- Begin by brainstorming flavors of ice cream that the children have had. Mark the containers in the freezer with these flavors.
- Make a flow chart that shows the steps in making a sundae. You might even have a book of pictures that show the steps involved in making all of the special ice cream treats.

Skills

Counting

- Make some of the ice cream scoops with sprinkles on them. Children can then count the sprinkles and place them in cones with the matching numeral on the cones.

Measuring

- Give students three types of the ice cream novelties that you made and a scale appropriate to their level (balance scale for younger children). Have them weigh each item and find which is heaviest and which is lightest.

Reading

- Write color words on the ice cream cones and have students place the correctly colored ice cream on top of the cone. Other cones can have the flavor words written on them (e.g., chocolate, vanilla).
- Cones can be made with number words on them, and students can use the scoops with the sprinkles on them and can place the scoop with the correct number of sprinkles on the cone with the number word.

Writing

- The children can make a chart of the flavors that are on special for the day.
- Students can invent a new flavor and write an ad to be placed in the center. They can also write a news release describing the reasons why someone should try this new flavor.

Using technology

- Have the children go online and see how many different flavors of ice cream they can find.

Other Ideas

- Offer the children different types of frozen products (e.g., ice milk, yogurt, ice cream) and have them taste all three. Talk about mouth feel, coldness, and overall taste. Repeat using sorbet, gelato, and sherbet. Make a graph or a Venn diagram from the tasting experiences and talk about the results.

- Have the children predict which will melt faster: ice milk, frozen yogurt, or ice cream. Have the children come up with a method for timing the melting (e.g., checking every 2 minutes).
- Bring in the ingredients and a recipe for making ice cream. Follow the recipe and place it in a crank ice cream maker to make it in class. Have students predict how long it will take. Talk about the role of the ice in the process. Children can also make their own bag ice cream (recipes and instructions can be found online).
- Make ice cream sundaes or banana splits in class.
- Observe dry ice and talk about the fact that dry ice is frozen carbon dioxide. Caution them not to touch the dry ice.

Book Connections

- Greenstein, E. (2003). *Ice cream cones for sale*. New York, NY: Arthur A. Levine.
- Page, J. (2002). *Clifford and the big ice cream mess*. New York, NY: Scholastic.
- Santoro, S. (1999). *Isaac the ice cream truck*. New York, NY: Holt.
- Snyder, I. (2003). *Milk to ice cream*. New York, NY: Children's Press.

Items That Families Might Donate or Loan to the Center

- empty ice cream containers (all sizes, but especially plastic quart ones)
- small single-serving ice cream containers
- empty containers of hot fudge and other types of sauces
- empty whipped cream containers
- small spoons

ICE CREAM PARLOR CENTER

PIZZA PARLOR CENTER

In this center, children will enjoy taking orders and assembling pizzas. The pizza parlor box should resemble a pizza oven. First, glue the lid to the box securely. Use a sharp knife to cut an oven door on one side of the box, making one long cut beneath the lid. Then cut downward at each corner to the bottom of the box. If you choose, you can make the shorter cuts downward about an inch from each corner instead of cutting along the box line (door cut; see Figure 1). The oven door should fold outward just like the door of a pizza oven. To protect the oven door, secure duct tape around the three raw edges. Then paint the box black (or charcoal gray).

If you would like to add a handle to the oven door, superglue a drawer handle onto the door at its center. Whatever contents you put inside the box can be taken out of the oven door when you need them.

When the center is used, place the oven on a table in an area of the classroom that will allow for dramatic play. Use another table or two to form a restaurant area. Other tables can serve as a counter for customers to order their pizzas or you can use another box. You might even consider designating one table for use as a salad bar. Decisions about the pizza parlor layout are based on the space you have available, but you can also consider asking students to design the center's floor plan. Their creative minds will surprise you with their inventiveness.

Contents

- vinyl tablecloth
- plastic flowers or a candle in a bottle
- pizza pans
- pizza shovel (fashion one out of a heavy piece of cardboard and paint it with silver spray paint)
- large cheese shaker and salt and pepper shakers
- an apron or two
- small rolling pin
- pizza cutter
- old pizza menus
- pizza boxes and napkins (request from a neighborhood pizza restaurant or clean boxes donated by families)
- pizza coupons from Sunday newspaper inserts
- round cardboard discs (purchase frozen pizza and clean the discs for classroom use, then spray the discs with clear varnish for durability and protection over time)

Content Information

- Talk to students about times when their families went to a pizza restaurant or ordered pizza to eat at home. Pizza is most often a favorite food with children, so this discussion should be lively.

- Tell students that the word *pizza* is Italian for "pie." We most often associate the food with Italy, although some evidence exists that pizzas were being eaten long before the Italians introduced them. Some people call them "pizza pies."
- Discuss how dough is made with yeast. Demonstrate how yeast rises by preparing dough, covering it, and allowing children to observe how it has become larger. Or ask for a family volunteer to come in and show children how pizza dough is made.
- Talk about the nutritional value of eating pizza (e.g., cheese has calcium that is good for building strong bones; vegetable toppings on pizzas are healthy choices). Remind students that pizza tends to be high in fat; therefore, it should not be eaten too often.
- If you think your children will enjoy a taste test, bring in focaccia bread for them to sample. Explain that *focaccia* is another Italian word.

Vocabulary Enrichment

- toppings
- pizza slices
- Italy/Italian
- fourths
- eighths
- sixteenths
- dough

- yeast
- toss
- waiter/waitress/server
- cook
- telephone order
- delivery

Dramatic Play/Cooperation

- Several roles for children's play are obvious: servers, pizza delivery boy or girl, chef, and customers. If you put play dough in the center, students can use the rolling pin to roll out pizza dough to place on pizza pans to "bake" in the oven. The pizza shovel should be available for putting the pizza in the oven and taking it out. They will need pencils and pads of paper to take orders from customers at the pizza parlor or by phone. If you become a customer in the pizza parlor, children's play becomes more interesting to them.

Skills

Counting

- Cut 10 round circles (perhaps 4–5 inches in diameter) from yellow poster board to resemble pizzas. Using markers, draw one piece of pepperoni sausage onto one of the circles, two pieces on a second circle, three pieces on a third circle, and so on, until you have all 10 circles marked. For easy visualization, prepare each pepperoni set using a traditional domino configuration. Children learn to recognize sets much more quickly when they are grouped together in a typical fashion. Students can put the circles in order from 1–10. Laminate your materials in order to use them from year to year.

Recognizing numerals

- To challenge students, use the circles described above and place numerals on the backside of each pizza. Children use numeral recognition to put the pizzas in order instead of the set configuration.

Counting by fives or tens

- Prepare 100 circle pizzas or more for older groups of children. With experience, first and second graders can put the pizzas into groups and count by fives or tens. This activity might also challenge more gifted preschool students.

Understanding fractions

- Use one round cardboard pizza disc as a base for developing a tool that will help children understand the concept of fourths, eighths, and sixteenths. Place three other cardboard discs that have been cut into pizza slices representing each of the fractions you are introducing on top of the first disc. For fun, suggest to students that they decorate the pizza slices using glue and scrap pieces of construction paper.

Auditory discrimination

- Using cardstock, prepare a set of durable picture cards that students can use to sort into two stacks: words that begin with /p/ and those that do not begin with /p/. Store these in an empty pizza box for children to use from year to year.

Throwing (or tossing)

- Show children how some pizza preparers throw pizza dough into the air to stretch it before putting it into the pizza pan (or ask your volunteer to demonstrate this experience). For the children's throwing activity, provide large round placemats that can be tossed into the air easily (and without injury to youngsters).

Other Ideas

- Use English muffins, pizza sauce, shredded cheese, and vegetable toppings to encourage children to make their own snacks. This activity can be organized for small groups or individual children can make their own during center time. The pizzas can be cooked in a small classroom toaster oven, or they can be taken to the school's kitchen and heated. Put the pizzas on wax paper so you can mark the paper with the children's names.

- For a group project, cut out one large circle from butcher paper and place it in the art center. Encourage groups of children to decorate the circle to look like a huge pizza, using markers, crayons, paint, or construction paper scraps that are glued to the paper.
- Conduct an in-class survey to determine which pizza choice is the most popular. If you teach in a large school, your students might want to conduct an in-school survey. After data are collected, print the results of the survey in the school's newsletter.

Book Connections

- Dobson, C. (2003). *Pizza counting.* Watertown, MA: Charlesbridge.
- Sturges, P. (2002). *The little red hen (makes a pizza).* New York, NY: Puffin.
- Walter, V. (1998). *"Hi, pizza man!"* New York, NY: Orchard Books.

That Families Might Donate or Loan to the Center

- discarded pizza boxes (or clean ones if a family has a connection to a pizza franchise)
- napkins and cups with franchise logos
- family volunteer who is willing to prepare pizza dough for your children's observation

FAST FOOD DRIVE-THROUGH CENTER

The box containing teaching aids for your fast food drive-through study does not need to be decorated, because an initial introduction to the center will ask your students to give their input about menu options and food costs. Write their recommendations on a poster the size of the box lid and glue the poster to the box for use as a menu board. As children brainstorm their entries, ask them to remember healthy choices they have seen at drive-through restaurants. Because of the disposable status of this poster, you can change it with each group of students you teach from year to year. The location of the center should be accessible to the art and home living centers in your classroom. A table or two will be necessary to promote children's play, because most fast food facilities provide for inside dining. The kitchen crew also needs a table for filling orders for their drive-through customers and the classroom cash register for making change.

Contents

- napkins, French fry containers, bags, cups, utensils, and other paraphernalia donated from a local fast food restaurant
- empty ketchup bottle (cleaned thoroughly)
- salt and pepper shakers
- table
- apron
- plastic food choices (burgers, hot dogs)
- teacher-made French fries
- salt, pepper, and catsup packets
- advertising circulars with coupons
- paper for wrapping products
- white bags
- plastic gloves
- scale
- classroom cash register
- carhop uniform and matching cap
- several feet of plastic tubing with funnels attached to both ends (to form a sound system for dramatic play opportunities)

Content Information

- Ask the children to name the fast food franchises they visit regularly. This conversation will help develop your menu. Talk to them about adding the cost of each menu item to the fast food menu board poster to assist in their dramatic play.
- Identify all of the types of fast food businesses available to students and their families: burgers, hot dogs, chicken, sandwiches, and seafood. Remember ethnic and cultural (e.g., Mexican, Cajun, German, Asian) food choices too.

- Explain that most fast food restaurants have sound systems that allow for ordering while looking at menu choices and prices shown on the menu board. Carhops are available at some eateries. Children might know that carhops occasionally wear roller skates.
- Talk about making healthy choices when going to fast food diners. If you have advertising circulars available that offer healthy food choices, show them to students and discuss their value for families who are concerned about their health.

Vocabulary Enrichment

- menu
- food choices
- order
- receipt
- catsup
- pickle
- relish
- tomato
- lettuce
- onion
- bun
- burgers
- hot dogs
- quarter-pounders
- submarine sandwiches
- fries
- onion rings
- shakes
- ice cream cones
- malts
- dipped cones
- cup holder
- bag
- microphone
- supersize
- beverage
- condiments
- straws
- ounces
- pounds
- carhop

Dramatic Play/Cooperation

- You can make French fry facsimiles by cutting yellow sponges into French fry strips. Or you can purchase plastic fast food products at teacher supply stores, through school supply catalogues, or online.
- Talk to students about making hamburgers, hot dogs, and other fast food using play dough or you can prepare samples using the salt dough recipe located in Appendix C.
- Children's pretend play can focus on ordering using the menu board and plastic tubing, then driving through to pick up their orders. Attach funnels to both ends of the tubing to improve sound production.
- Children who are in the fast food kitchen should be prepared to fill customer orders accurately.

FAST FOOD DRIVE-THROUGH CENTER

FAST FOOD DRIVE-THROUGH CENTER

Skills

Ordering

- Place empty beverage cups in the manipulatives center for students to put in order from smallest to largest. Share with them the relative sizes of the cups (e.g., 16-ounce, 24-ounce, 36-ounce). Introduce the term *supersize*, explaining that fast food restaurants prefer to sell larger drinks to increase their sales. Remind students that larger sizes often have higher calories and sugar content.

Weighing objects

- Use play dough in the art center for children to make hamburger patties and hot dogs. Tell children that fast food diners weigh their food before cooking it to ensure that all food choices weigh the same. Place the classroom scale in the fast food center, suggesting an appropriate weight for each hamburger or hot dog (e.g., 4 ounces). Explain to students that they have to make the items heavier or lighter if the weight is not accurate.

Scientific observation

- Bring in two or three popular brands of potato chips and place samples of each on paper towels. After a few hours (or overnight), check the grease residue that has seeped onto each towel. Ask children which brand might be the healthiest eating choice. Tell children that grease often indicates a high fat content.

Alliteration

- Point out to children that local fast food restaurants have names such as Hamburger Heaven or Hot Dog Hangout. Encourage them to use their own names to create a business for themselves such as Emily's Eatery, Nick's Nuggets, Lauren's Lunchbox, Shelly's Sandwich Shop, Dylan's Deli, or Madison's Munchies. For students' whose names are difficult to find alliterative matches, suggest they try their last names instead.

Literary elements

- Follow up the alliteration activity by asking children to develop advertising jingles for their fast food establishment, such as "Jack's Shakes Are Cool!," "Ally's Food Is Awesome!," "Try Maddie's Sandwich Melts!," or "Zoey's Burgers Are Zesty-licious!"

Identifying media influences

- Show children fast food advertising flyers or view a television video clip of families eating at a fast food restaurant and discuss the components of each that are designed to attract customers to buy their products.

Other Ideas

- Suggest to students that they can make fast food posters. Place fast food circulars in the art center for them to tear or cut out pictures of their favorite foods to glue onto the posters. They should write their names on the posters and display them on a bulletin board in the classroom.
- Children can also make fast food coupons to get special prices when they use the classroom fast food drive-through. Or, if they prefer, they can make paper money.
- Prepare hot dogs for lunch one day during the fast food study. Have a variety of condiments available for students to dress their own dogs. Some might prefer chili and onions, too.
- Place large chocolate cookies (or chocolate graham crackers) and slightly melted ice cream on the snack tables so children can prepare ice cream sandwich treats for afternoon snack time. Put these in sandwich bags, marking them with children's names, and store them in a freezer until serving time.
- Remind students that trash from fast food restaurants needs to be tossed into public garbage receptacles or taken home to put into the waste can at home. Organize a litter clean up day for your school's playground. Give students plastic gloves and trash bags and help them remove unwanted objects from your play area.

Book Connections

- Freymann, S., & Elffers, J. (2006). *Fast food*. New York, NY: Arthur A. Levine.

Items That Families Might Donate or Loan to the Center

- empty cup containers (cleaned)
- sandwich bags
- fast food advertising circulars
- plastic gloves
- trash bags
- a carhop costume (if families have one they are willing to lend)

Chapter 10 Transportation Theme Centers

Transportation units abound in early childhood classrooms, so these centers will have a natural fit into most curriculums. Although the topics will appeal to many boys just because of the materials, girls will also enjoy the materials and varied activities included in each center. After seeing how these centers are accepted in your classroom, you could expand on these centers and develop other ones based upon the interests of your children. Boats, trains, and spaceships would be other possible centers.

RACETRACK CENTER

This box can be made to look like the stands at a racetrack. Spray paint the outside of the box with a dark color. Make a mural of people in the stands on one of the long sides of the box. Cut the box's back two corners, so that the back of the box can be lowered. Then cut along the sides from the bottom back to the front, so that the sides can be moved out (one open side cut; see Figure 2). This will allow the children to more easily get to the inside of the box for the activities that will be done there. Garage doors may be cut into the bottoms of the sides by making two cuts about 3 inches apart and 4 inches up. Fold up the door to open.

On the inside bottom of the box, you will need to draw parking spaces. Then cover the bottom of the box with clear contact paper. You can number the parking spaces with the numbers from the cars using an erasable marker. Spaces may be renumbered and even number words may be used. By doing this, you can change the activities and make them either harder or easier, depending upon your students' abilities. Use a corrugated cardboard piece that is about 12 inches wide by 3 feet long for a ramp for racing cars. Draw a line down the middle of the entire ramp. Attach the ramp to one of the sides of the "stands" box with masking tape. You may need to support your ramp with a large block underneath to keep it from sagging. Your ramp is now complete.

For the actual racetrack, cut a piece of black butcher paper, black plastic, or fabric that is approximately 16 inches by 3 feet. Draw or paint an oval on this and draw or paint a line down the middle. This is your racetrack. If you use butcher paper, be sure to laminate it so it will last. The track can be rolled for storage in the box.

Another piece of brown or gray paper that is approximately 12 inches by 2 feet will be the parking lot for the facility. Draw parking spaces on this and laminate it. The spaces can be marked with a permanent marker in several ways: "longest car," "shortest car," "red car." Using an erasable marker on top of the lamination allows you the opportunity to make changes in the parking lot as needed to meet the needs of your students.

Contents

- small cars with and without numbers on them
- road signs (print and glue them to flat wooden toothpicks stuck into Styrofoam)
- flags that signal the start and finish of the race
- toy cars that can be assembled and disassembled or cars with missing parts
- wheels
- balance scale
- small figures of police officers and drivers

Content Information

- Racetracks are places where people can race in cars. They will have a set number of laps in the race and the car that finishes first is the winner.
- The cars are specially adapted for racing, will have a number on them, and will be sponsored by a company.
- Drivers receive special training before they become racecar drivers.
- The cars will have to visit the pit during the race for gas and to have the tires changed.
- Flags are used to communicate with the drivers. A green flag is given at the start. A yellow flag means no passing, as there has been an accident. A checkered flag means you are the winner.
- The people sit in the grandstand and watch the race. The stands are like a stadium and have food and restrooms available.

Vocabulary Enrichment

- lap
- grandstand
- pit and pit crew
- tire rotation
- miles per hour (mph)
- sponsor
- speedway
- spectators
- fuel
- roll
- checkered flag
- muffler

Dramatic Play/Cooperation

- Before introducing the center, read a couple of books about car racing to the students, showing pictures of a racetrack and pointing out the different areas. This is a good way to provide the children with the information they need for dramatic play.
- Full-size dramatic play is best done outside. The children can make racecars out of paper. They can choose the number for their car and their sponsor and decorate it as they wish. Pin the cars on their shirts. One child can be the flag person. The racetrack needs to be defined by the teacher. Have the cars walk the track before the race so that they know where they will be driving. Other children can pretend to be selling hot dogs, sodas, popcorn, and other items. The spectators can sit along the track. The cars then run along the track.

RACETRACK CENTER

RACETRACK CENTER

Skills

Counting

- A sign can be posted that tells how many empty parking spots are available in the parking lot.
- Tires can be counted into bins.

Sorting

- Spare tires can be sorted according to size, type, or some other characteristic.

Matching

- The children can match tires to the cars that have tires missing.

Ordering from shortest to longest

- Parking spaces can be marked for shortest to longest cars, and students will have to arrange the cars accordingly.

Weighing

- Using a selection of cars and a balance scale, the children can weigh and arrange the cars from lightest to heaviest.
- Older or more advanced students can use postal scales and actually record the weight of the cars.

Measuring

- Older or more advanced students can use rulers to measure the cars and make a graph showing how many cars are a particular length.

Number words

- Write number words on the parking spaces. The children can read the words and find the car with the corresponding numerals on it.

Writing numerals

- Students can gain practice in writing numerals as they write numerals in specific parking spaces for the cars.

Writing

- Have the children write road signs and/or directions for the center.
- Students can make posters promoting their racecar as the best.
- After playing with the center for several days, the children can each write a page for a class book on car racing.

Art

- Children can design new cars on paper.

Other Ideas

- Use the Internet to "visit" some of the nationally known racetracks.
- Let the children have car races down a 6-foot-long board ramp.
- If money is no object, you can buy some of the Cub Scout pine wood derby cars. Let the children put them together and decorate their car. You can

either have small groups for each car or individual cars. Ask parents and other adults to help you with this activity.

- Use a toy radar gun and clock cars going by your school. Clock the children running and throwing a ball. Compare their fastest times to the speed of the average racecar (more than 100 miles an hour).

Book Connections

- Herzog, B. (2006). *R is for race: A stock car alphabet*. Chelsea, MI: Sleeping Bear Press.
- Rex, M. (2000). *My race car*. New York, NY: Scholastic.
- Zane, A. (2005). *Wheels on the race car*. New York, NY: Orchard.

Items That Families Might Donate or Loan to the Center

- auto parts (that have no sharp edges) for the discovery table in the classroom
- small cars with missing parts

RACETRACK CENTER

CAR CARE CENTER

Paint the car care center box and its lid any color you prefer. When the box is dry, attach different car parts that have been cut from construction paper and laminated. Place two tires (black circles) on each of the long sides of the box with superglue. Add headlights (yellow or gray circles) and a hood ornament on one end of the box. Fashion windshield wipers using pipe cleaners, bending them so that they can be attached with duct tape on the inside of the box. Pipe cleaners are flexible enough that they can be moved back and forth if children choose to simulate this action. Use markers to add other features you think are appropriate.

Set up the car care center near the block center, because blocks can be arranged so that students have a service bay for their dramatic play. Visit a local junkyard and purchase a steering wheel, an old tire, windshield wipers, rearview mirror, a hood ornament or two, a seatbelt, and a spark plug from vehicles that have been involved in accidents. You will not be able to place these purchases in your car care center box because of their size, but you can retain them in your home or in a storage area of your school. The dramatic play will be richer if you have at least one wheeled toy in your classroom.

Contents

- car brochures (visit local car dealerships to request brochures about older models)
- toy car and truck models
- old license plate
- outdated inspection sticker
- empty oilcan (cleaned thoroughly)
- empty car wax container
- spark plug
- map
- hood ornament or two
- keys and key chains
- chamois
- photographs of vehicles and speed limit and traffic signs
- tire pressure gauge
- tire jack

Content Information

- Talk about all of the reasons that vehicles might need service (e.g., the battery has gone dead, a tire is flat, someone has had an accident) and ask students to share a story when their family has had problems with their transportation.
- Describe the need for oil changes and regular checkups that drivers need to keep their vehicles running smoothly. Use the term *maintenance* and tell children that a regular schedule of maintenance helps keep vehicles running smoothly for a much longer time.

CAR CARE CENTER

- Define the role of the speedometer in vehicles. Once children understand speed limit signs, they can remind drivers to slow down if they are speeding.
- Demonstrate the use of seatbelts. Remind students that states have laws about seatbelt use and that they should use always their seatbelts when they get into vehicles.

Vocabulary Enrichment

- car
- truck
- vehicle
- automobile
- hood
- trunk
- brakes
- steering wheel
- speedometer
- battery
- rearview mirror
- side view mirror
- sun visor
- seatbelt
- infant seat
- airbag
- floor mats
- mechanic
- garage
- service manager
- tire
- flat
- inflate
- tire jack
- wheel alignment
- engine
- spark plug
- pistons
- gears
- hydraulic lift
- oil change
- maintenance schedule
- wrecker
- hood ornament
- global positioning system (GPS)
- map
- driver's license
- inspection sticker
- carwash
- car wax
- gasoline
- gas station
- price per gallon
- hybrid car

Dramatic Play/Cooperation

- Having an initial discussion with students about the function and operations of a car care center and adding a steering wheel and tire to your classroom block center will spur children's play activity. Include several miniature cars and trucks for children's use.
- Place a seatbelt in the car care center, demonstrate how to use it, and observe students using it in their play.
- If you have large wheeled toys in your classroom, suggest to students that they can wash them on the playground. Facilitate the play with a chamois

CAR CARE CENTER

CAR CARE CENTER

and pail of water. Children can also paint a large wheeled toy with washable paint that can be removed at a later date.

Skills

Tracing

- Place car and truck stencils in the art center. Request that students trace and cut out patterns to display on a classroom bulletin board.
- Use keys as stencils. Children can trace keys and cut them out. Tell children that drivers have to know where their keys are at all times. Ask them to carry their keys with them for a specified period of time (perhaps an hour). Ask them to describe their reactions to the responsibility of taking care of their keys.

Writing

- Tell children that employees who work in car care centers wear shirts that have their names on them. Provide disposable nametags for children to write their names and place the tag on their clothing when they participate in dramatic play in this center.
- Show students what an inspection sticker is and tell them why drivers need them on their automobiles. Ask them to use supplies in the writing center to make an inspection sticker for the wheeled toys in the classroom.
- Show children your driver's license, telling them that drivers have to have them in order to drive in your state. Encourage each student to create his or her own driver's license and require students to have one to drive any of the wheeled toys in your classroom.

Spatial relationships

- Show children a map and explain why drivers need directions to find their destinations. Ask small groups of children to prepare a map that shows how to get from the classroom to another part of your building (e.g., cafeteria, library) or playground. Explain to children that many vehicles now have global positioning systems (GPS) in them, so some families will not use maps.
- Bring in a GPS unit. Allow students to experiment with it in pedestrian mode.

Subtraction

- Formulate word problems that require children to subtract two-digit numbers (appropriate for second graders). Once children have had experience with these subtraction problems, encourage them to develop their own word problems. Here are a few examples:
  o If you are driving 40 miles per hour in a school zone with a posted speed limit of 20 miles per hour, how far over the speed limit are you driving?

o When you drive 45 miles per hour in a posted speed limit zone of 60 miles per hour, how far below the speed limit are you going?

o What is the difference in speed between 35 miles per hour and 50 miles per hour?

o If someone is driving 65 miles per hour in a 50-mile-per-hour speed zone, how far over the speed limit is he going?

Understanding puns

- Second graders usually enjoy the fun in puns. Suggest to children that they develop some puns of their own related to the center. Here are a few examples:
  o "Wheel" take a trip in the car.
  o "Orange" you glad you have a car?
  o I "tire" on long trips.
  o I "car" for you.
  o We "auto" clean up the room soon.
  o Car parts can "brake."

Other Ideas

- Using salt dough, ask students to make at least four tires each. When they are cooked, paint them black. Then count them or group them into sets. Remember to organize one set to represent an 18-wheeler.
- During the car care center study, use the well-known tune "The Wheels on the Bus" to sing verses about a car:

    The pistons on the car go ping, ping, ping;
    Ping, ping, ping; ping, ping, ping;
    The pistons on the car go ping, ping, ping;
    All around the town.
    Other verses you can use are:
    The horn on the car goes honk, honk, honk.
    The gears on the car roll round and round.
    The tires on the car go whirr, whirr, whirr.

    Ask children to suggest other verses as they gain knowledge about vehicles.
- Place funnels in the water table. Fill an empty oilcan with water for students to pour into the funnel. Or use funnels in the sand table, filling the oil can with sand. Show a photograph of a mechanic pouring oil into the engine.
- Start a special category on the classroom word wall titled "Vehicles." Children (with assistance from their families) can generate words related to this throughout the ongoing study of the car care center including: *automobile,*

CAR CARE CENTER

CAR CARE CENTER

car, sedan, station wagon, ambulance, taxi, police car, truck, bus, van, limousine, wrecker, convertible, sports utility vehicle (SUV), 18-wheeler, armored car, armored truck, motorcycle, racecar, and others they recommend. If automobile company names are suggested, use these words, too, because the intent of the word wall is children's understanding of print. Remind children that all of these vehicles need service from car care centers.

- When the car care study is winding down, talk to students about art cars and suggest that they create art cars in small groups and have an art car parade. Bring in large boxes that families donate and encourage children to decorate them with all types of art materials. Small paper plates are useful for representing tires and headlights. If you remove the bottoms of each box, students will be able to slip them over their heads and carry them in the parade. Or you can attach heavy ribbon or rope onto the box corners (as if they were suspenders) and children will have their hands free as they parade. Lead a parade through the school, or invite families into the classroom to view the fun.

Book Connections
- Aylmore, A. (2007). *I like cars.* Portsmouth, NH: Heinemann/Raintree.
- Blair, S. (2008). *Isabel's car wash.* New York, NY: Albert Whitman.

Items That Families Might Donate or Loan to the Center
- commercial car and truck brochures
- magazines
- old license plate
- outdated inspection sticker
- empty oilcan (cleaned thoroughly)
- empty car wax container
- map
- hood ornament or two
- keys and key chains
- spark plugs
- chamois
- several large boxes

AIRPORT CENTER

The layout for this center will be similar to the racetrack center: Place the box on the table and remove the lid. On one of the long sides at both corners, you will need to cut down from the top edge to the bottom, freeing this side (one open side cut; see Figure 2). Fold the long side out. Paint the box to look like a terminal or find a picture of a terminal and glue it to the outside of the remaining long side of the box. Name your airport and write the name in large letters across the top of this side. On each of the short sides, cut double doors into the terminal. If you want to get really detailed, make counters, departure and arrival screens, and a baggage claim area. These can be fashioned out of small boxes.

If you bought black vinyl for the racetrack, check the backside to see if you can use it for the airport runways. Sometimes the back is either black or gray. Either of these will work for your tarmac. Paint two runways on the vinyl. If you check the layout of airports, you will see that two runways will not be parallel to each other because planes have to take off into the wind. You can also use the parking lot from the racetrack center. You will also need a control tower. A long, rectangular box set on its end will serve as the tower. It can be painted and windows can be cut out at the top and covered with clear plastic.

Contents

- small planes
- fire trucks, ambulances, and helicopters for emergency vehicles
- cars from the racetrack center and its parking lot
- drawstring bags or small plastic boxes that have a closing lid can be used like suitcases
- maps of the United States
- catalogues, store sales brochures, and index cards (children cut out the items they will pack and glue them onto the index cards)
- dry erase markers
- ruler
- sticky notes
- used boarding passes

Content Information

- Airplanes carry people and cargo around the world.
- Airports have terminals, runways, taxiways, and control towers.
- Jobs in the airport include pilot, copilot, flight attendant, baggage handler, security people, and ground crew.
- You have to have a boarding pass to get on the plane. The boarding pass will have a seat assignment printed on it. That is the seat assigned to you.
- Planes come in different sizes and have different seat arrangements.

AIRPORT CENTER

Vocabulary Enrichment

- runway
- parallel
- taxiway
- terminal
- control tower
- tram
- air traffic control
- commercial flights
- first class
- business class
- coach
- maintenance
- tarmac
- Federal Aviation Administration (FAA)
- customs
- immigration
- docking
- ground crew
- cargo
- flight attendant
- pilot
- copilot
- baggage
- baggage handlers
- security
- radar
- approach
- originating
- terminating
- docking

Dramatic Play/Cooperation

- Bring in small suitcases and have them available for the children to pack with doll clothes or dress up clothes.
- Old boarding passes could be used at the gate, and one area of the classroom could have a few chairs arranged for the inside of the plane.
- If you have a small audio/visual cart in your classroom, this could be used as the drink cart. Plastic cups for pretend drinks could be used from the camping center.

Skills

Number words

- Take the planes and write number words on them. Then have the children park the planes in parking spaces on the tarmac that have the written numeral on the space.

Sums to 10

- Sums to 10 can be practiced by making 10 small runways on construction paper. Laminate them. Print addition problems on the computer, cut them out and laminate them. Have the children place a problem on the runway and use small planes to model the problem. If the runways are laminated, the children can use a dry erase marker to write the answer on the runway.

Multiplication foundations

- Multiplication can be taught and reinforced by using the wheels on the planes to show groups of two. Cars can show groups of four and helicopters with two rotors can show groups of three.

Initial sounds

- Give students index cards with the first letter of an item that might be packed in a suitcase for a trip. For example, "p" could be placed on a card. The children can look through sales brochures and catalogues, find an item that begins with a "p" (such as pants) that could be packed, cut it out, glue it on the index card, and write the word.

Estimating weights

- Make little boxes look like suitcases (all alike so that the children can't memorize the answers by looking at them). Place differing amounts of washers in the boxes. Glue these shut. Tell the children that the weight limit for the bags on your mini airline is 4 ounces. They will sort the bags into groups according to whether they think the bags are overweight or not. They can then check their choices using a postal scale.

Cardinal directions

- Have students make radar screens using a compass or by tracing around a circle. Have them mark their screens with north, north northeast, east, south southeast, south, south southwest, west, and north northwest. Have a map of the United States and place laminated airplanes coming into an airport near you. Number the airplanes. Have the children record the direction of the planes on a clipboard. If you attach the planes with tape, you can move them around on the map each day.

Map skills

- Laminate a map of the United States. Give the children a dry erase marker and a scale that you have made. One inch might equal 100 miles. Make cards that have flights originating from different cities and landing in other cities (e.g., Flight 53 is leaving Chicago and flying to New York). The children will take the dry erase marker and draw a line between the two cities. They will then measure the line, compare it to the scale, and record on a sticky note the distance between the two cities. They will place the sticky note on the map. You can use these sticky notes to spot check for understanding by measuring the distance yourself.

Reading a diagram

- Print, enlarge, and laminate several diagrams from various airlines seat selection menus. Write seat assignments on sticky notes and have students locate seats and place the sticky note on the correct seat on the plane. Be sure to have planes that have different arrangements inside.

Airplane design

- Let students make a paper airplane and fly it in the classroom. See which plane goes the farthest. Let them try modifications to the plane to see if they can get it to go further (e.g., adding a tail, adding weight). Older children can measure the distance their plane actually flew.

Writing and reading

- Provide a box with doll clothes, small samples of toothpaste, and other items commonly taken on a trip. Pictures will also work, if you don't want to provide actual items. Have one child make a list of everything that he wants to take on a trip. Let him give his list to another child to pack the suitcase.

Other Ideas

- Take a field trip to an airport. If a large airport is not close to you, see if a small airport will allow you to visit. Small airports would be more likely to let the children actually see inside a plane. Or, using the Internet, take your students on a virtual tour of an airport (search for "airport virtual tour"). This would be a great introduction to your center.
- Find songs that are about airplanes. Teach the children the songs. Write the words on a large chart for the children to follow along as they sing.
- Weather can be a problem for planes. Talk to students about different weather conditions that would ground a plane.
- Make a windsock and fly it outside your classroom window, if possible. Have the children look at the windsock and tell the direction of the wind.
- Buy parachute men at a party store, enough for groups of three or four children to have four parachutes per group. Leave one chute the way it is. Cut a one-inch hole in the top of another chute. Replace the man on the third chute with something that is more spread out (those cheap frogs that jump work well), and for the final chute, remove the man and attach a small plastic bathroom cup to the chute. Have the children predict if the two men will fall at the same rate or not and if the hole in the chute makes a difference. Let them test their hypothesis. Now have them compare the frog to one of the men. Finally, ask them if they think there is a point where a parachute will not work. Tell them to now take the chute with the cup and the supply of washers (from the hardware store) and keep adding one washer at a time. How many washers did it take before the chute doesn't float but just falls?
- Be sure and ask if anyone in your students' families knows someone associated with an airline. If so, that person might come to your class, send items to your class, or make arrangements with the airline for your class to visit it at the airport.

Book Connections

- Barton, B. (1987). *Airport*. New York, NY: HarperCollins.
- Hill, M. (2003). *Signs at the airport*. New York, NY: Children's Press.
- Scarry, R. (2001). *Richard Scarry's A day at the airport*. New York, NY: Random House.
- Sharmat, M. W. (1990). *Gila monsters meet you at the airport*. New York, NY: Aladdin.

Items That Families Might Donate or Loan to the Center

- old boarding passes or itineraries from a trip
- catalogues
- store brochures
- spare hardware washers

AIRPORT CENTER

Chapter 11

Special Interest Centers

This section offers you a few choices of centers that children find especially appealing. Be aware that your children are different from year to year. A center that is very popular one year may not be popular the next year. The children's interests should be respected if you want to maximize their learning at any one center.

You might find your children captivated by bugs one year. Use these examples as a starting point for developing other special interest centers for your children. The list of new centers that you could develop for your children has no limits. If they are interested in a topic, you can make a center. Some other topics you might consider here are astronomy, other cultures, other countries, insects, and snakes.

AMERICAN INDIAN CENTER

Even though your children might have had a unit about American Indians in a previous grade, the things that you will be doing with them here will, more than likely, be at a much greater depth and will include activities that they have not done before.

This box will have two sides for activities. With the box on the table, take off the lid. On the short sides, draw a line down from the middle of the top edge to the bottom. Cut down this line on both short sides. At the bottom of the box on the short sides, cut the box from the first cut along the bottom to the corners, freeing the short sides. Fold these side pieces out (open ends cut; see Figure 4). With the side flaps folded out, you will have two different work areas for the children, as they sit in front of each long side. One side can be painted to resemble the plains and the other side can be painted to resemble woodlands. Plains scenery can have mesas and mountains. The woodlands side should have forests drawn on the box.

The children can make many of the items for use with the box. Using cone cups that are near many water coolers, have the children decorate and make these into tepees. The tepees can be placed on tan felt or brown butcher paper that will become the plains ground and be spread in front of the plains scene. The lodges can be placed on green felt or green butcher paper to represent the ground of the woodlands. You can make lodges by cutting the bottoms out of 2-liter drink bottles. Cut them so that they are about 3 inches tall. Discard the top part of the bottle. Cut a rounded door. Have the children tear brown paper sacks and glue them on the outside, overlapping the pieces. These will be used in the woodlands scene.

In addition to these items for the center, provide the children with books that include many pictures of scenes from American Indian life and let the children make additional items for each side of the box using art materials.

Contents

- plastic Indians and horses
- small sticks and rocks
- acorns
- baskets
- dried corn
- artificial animal skins/similar fabric
- paper feathers

- arrowhead replicas
- beads
- self-hardening clay
- yarn
- markers
- pencils
- feather stencils
- colored paper

Content Information

- Tell students why the American Indians were first called Indians.
- Explain what a tribe is and how the area where the tribe lived determined the type of house the Indians made, what foods they had to eat, and whether or not they were nomadic.
- Explain why some tribes had to be nomadic.
- Choose the vocabulary that you are going to focus on and talk about those words and their definitions.

Vocabulary Enrichment

- tribes
- arrowheads
- shards
- indigenous
- reservation
- hogan
- tepee
- lodge
- long house
- medicine man
- shaman
- brave
- warrior
- papoose
- travois
- wampum
- pueblo
- drumming
- rattles

- sandpainting
- nomadic
- turquoise
- cradleboard
- weaving
- pottery
- maize
- grinding stone
- serrated
- obsidian
- flakes
- projectile points
- scraper
- effigy pieces
- moccasin
- pestle
- metate
- awl

Dramatic Play/Cooperation

- A large tepee may be made by rolling newspapers into poles. Open the newspaper sections and lay about four sheets of newspaper in lines that overlap every four pages by about 3/4 of the paper. Start at the top corner and roll the newspapers, adding four sheet sections until you get the length you need. Tape the newspapers closed with masking tape along the pole where the ends hang out. Make three or four poles and use these as the poles for the tepee. Paper grocery sacks can be cut down one side and the bottom cut out. This will form a large rectangle. The children can decorate them with

AMERICAN INDIAN CENTER

Indian signs. You can punch holes into the sides and then string together the sides to form a large blanket. Your students can do some of the weaving. Place this around your poles and weave it closed at the top. You now have a tepee. This tepee will stand for 4–6 weeks before collapsing, depending upon use.

- You can add store-bought Indian headdresses, moccasins, leggings, and shawls for the children to wear.
- The dolls may be wrapped onto cradleboards made of cardboard with strips of cloth.
- Baskets, plastic fruits, acorns, and dried corn could be added for gathering.
- If a parent has loaned you a grinding stone (metate), you can bring in dried corn for the students to grind. You can get corn from a feed store, but be sure that it hasn't been treated. Seed corn often is pretreated with chemicals. You will want to purchase feed corn.

Skills

Counting

- Have a large number of feathers already cut out of colored construction paper. Have students place specified amounts of feathers on pictures of headdresses that are missing feathers. The numeral can be listed on the headdress band or the number word can be used for a more challenging task.

Tracing and cutting

- Cardboard stencils of feathers can be supplied for the children to trace and cut out.

Reading

- For older or more advanced children, write out instructions on how to make an Indian bonnet. They will then read and follow the directions. For example, the directions could tell the children to trace 10 feathers in the following colors: three red, two yellow, four orange, and one gray. Do not make a sample of the final product or the children will just look at it and not read the directions.
- Because Indians depended upon hunting game for food, they needed to know how to identify animals by their tracks. Bring in pictures of animal tracks and a book on identifying animals from their tracks. Let students work on identifying the prints.

Fine-motor development

- Weaving: Using the bottoms of milk jugs that are cut so that the sides around the bottom are about 1 1/2 inches tall, cut 1/3 inch cuts down the two sides that are opposite each other. The cuts should be about 1/3 of an inch apart. This makes your loom. The yarn will be attached to these top and bottom slits. The children will weave the yarn over and under these strings as they go from side to side. When finished, you will need to tie off the ends and remove it from the loom for the younger children.

- Beads can be provided for stringing. Very tiny beads can be used with older children. If you can find samples or pictures of items that the American Indians made using beads, the children could see how advanced their beadwork was. It is often possible to buy beadwork items at cultural centers and online. You can find everything from beaded hairclips to bottles entirely covered with tiny beads strung in designs.

Weighing

- Using arrowheads that are close in size, have the children use a scale to determine which one is the heaviest. They can put them in order from heaviest to lightest.

Map skills

- Using a large map of the United States, provide pictures of different Indian homes and tribe names and have children try to place the Indians in the correct area on the map. Provide an answer key map for the children to check their work.

Counting to five in Choctaw

- The children can be taught simple words from the Choctaw language or one of the other American Indian Nations' languages. Counting words are always of interest to the children. Many of them will know how to count in Spanish from watching TV programs. These words are the Choctaw words for one to five: *achuffa* (one), *tuklo* (two), *tuchina* (three), *ushta* (four), and *tahlapi* (five).

Art

- Have paper and markers available for the children to design a headband using real American Indian signs and designs.
- Make colored sand by using food dye and sand. Allow the sand to dry. (If you prefer, you can buy colored sand.) Talk to students about how the shaman used sand in sand painting. Give students a piece of white cardboard. Have them use white glue to make a design and then sprinkle the colored sand on it the same way that they would use glitter.
- Self-hardening clay can be purchased at craft stores. Some Indian pots were made by making ropes and placing them around a base. The sides of the pot were then smoothed out. After students make their pots, allow them to harden. Collect some pine straw and fashion a brush by taping several pieces of pine straw together. Let the students decorate their clay pots using poster paints or paint from the art center.

AMERICAN INDIAN CENTER

Other Ideas

- American Indian words are readily available on websites. The children can learn to count in one of the languages. They can compare the words for the numbers of several of the tribes. Sites often include a pronunciation key for the words.
- Talk about how sound carries through the ground. Begin by having students put their heads down on a table and have one child tap on the table. Talk about how the Indians could put their ear to the ground and hear horses coming. Have some of the children put their ears on the floor and ask others to jump up and down. Can they hear the sounds? Take them outside and have them experiment. Can they hear any sounds? Have some children run and jump up and down near them. Now can they hear the sounds?
- It was important for Indians to walk quietly. First, as students walk down the hall, tell them to listen. Now challenge them to walk without making any noise whatsoever. You can also take the children outside and let them try to walk without making any noise through leaves and sticks. Blindfold one child and have another child try to sneak up on him. The blindfolded child has to say when he hears the other child and point to the direction that the sound comes from.
- Invite an American Indian to come talk to your class.
- Older or more advanced children can be given an Indian tribe to research. They can make posters to share what they learned with the class.
- Invite an amateur archeologist to come to your class and share with the children how she got started collecting. (In rural areas, when farmers plow their fields in the spring and after a rain, you can walk through the field with your eyes on the ground and find pottery shards and even arrowheads, if the Indians had a village there.) If she has a collection, she can bring it to share with the children.
- Read books to the children that deal with events in the everyday lives of the Indians.

Book Connections

- dePaola, T. (1996). *The legend of the Indian paintbrush*. New York, NY: Putnam Juvenile.
- dePaola, T. (2002). *The legend of the bluebonnet*. New York, NY: Putnam Juvenile.
- Fronval, G. (1991). *Indian signals and sign language*. New York, NY: Random House.

Items That Families Might Donate or Loan to the Center

- arrowheads, blankets, grinding stones, pottery shards, books on American Indians, or any other items related to American Indians (They might have purchased souvenirs during their travels they are willing to loan. Valuable items should not come to school without the parent and other items can be placed in your shadow box display case and locked up for protection.)

- leftover yarn for weaving projects
- empty, clean one-gallon milk jugs
- empty, clean 2-liter drink bottles
- paper grocery sacks

AMERICAN INDIAN CENTER

FARM AND FARM SUPPLY CENTER

The farm and farm supply center should resemble a barn. Paint the box red with a contrasting color for the lid (brown or yellow). On one side of the box, cut a door that will open outward. Use markers to draw other barn features (e.g., windows, shutters, air vents, upper level doors). Children should use the box when they play with farm people and farm animal figurines.

Some regions of the country provide rich farmland for growing crops, while others consist of large acres of prairie land more appropriate for ranching. As you plan your farm and farm supply center study, think about the types of farms in your community. Will you focus on large farms that grow only one crop (e.g., corn, wheat, avocados)? Or do farmers in your area grow several crops to sell in farmers' markets? Are there dairy farms in your state or pig and poultry farms? Some farmers stock ponds with fish to sell to local vendors.

Some of your children's family members may work in plants or factories that process canned foods, while others work in companies that package fresh foods to sell. Having some preliminary knowledge about farms in your community helps children understand the relevance of the study.

Contents

- farm set (including farm people figurines and farm animal figurines)
- small tractor (and other farm machinery, if available)
- farmer's hat, pair of overalls, kerchief, and colorful shirt (to construct a scarecrow)
- wind chime
- samples of food for cattle, horses, and other animals (stored in zipper bags)
- animal feed sacks
- seed packets
- farm animal stencils

- a sample of barb wire (also called barbed wire in some regions)
- pictures of various types of farms
- empty milk product containers (cleaned thoroughly)
- child-sized gardening tools
- bird feeder or rabbit hutch
- aluminum bucket
- small baskets for produce
- toy cash register
- short rope
- horse fly mask (if it is available, explain its use to your children)
- scale

Content Information

- Talk to children about all of the types of farms that exist in the country, pointing out the specific farms that are prevalent in your county or parish. Help children understand that the foods we eat are grown on farms, processed in special companies and factories, and delivered to the grocery stores in our community.

- Point out that some of the food we purchase at grocery stores is fresh. Tell children that fresh food is sold in the *produce* section. Discuss with children that some of our food is grown locally and sold to grocery stores or in farmers' markets.
- Describe the basic components of farming (e.g., tilling the soil, planting seeds, watering plants, pulling weeds, eliminating plant predators, harvesting the crop). Tell children that farmers with large farms hire people (called *hired hands*) to assist during each step of the farming process.
- Talk about the need that large farms have for irrigation systems to water their plants. Bring in a soaker hose, briefly demonstrating its use on the playground.
- Define the role of the farm supply store (or tractor supply store) in supporting farmers in their work. These stores are much like department stores for farmers because of the variety of supplies they provide for their customers.

Vocabulary Enrichment

- farmer
- farmer's wife
- hired hands
- plants
- seeds
- garden
- field
- orchard
- vegetables
- organic
- milk
- milk products
- milking machine
- farmers' market
- produce
- cistern
- auction
- horse
- cow

- cattle
- pigs
- hogs
- swine
- tractors
- plow
- tillers
- threshing machines
- combines
- fertilizer
- irrigation system
- farm and feed store
- tractor supply store
- trough
- hutch
- scarecrow
- work dog
- harvest

FARM AND FARM SUPPLY CENTER

163

Dramatic Play/Cooperation

- Set up a classroom farmers' market (described under artistic expression in the skills section) or grocery store for dramatic play opportunities.
- The farm set and the barn box will serve as an impetus for farm and farm supply play.
- Talk to children about the scarecrow's function (to frighten birds away from crops as they are growing). Suggest that they use the clothing in the box to build a scarecrow, stuffing the overalls and shirt with hay. Hang a wind chime near an open window or door, explaining to children that wind chimes have a similar purpose as a scarecrow.

Skills

Artistic expression

- Provide materials in the art center for children to create papier-mâché fruits and vegetables. Show students how to wad newspapers into small balls and layer strips of newspaper around the ball with a watery paste (or you can use masking tape). When the art products are dry, paint them with tempera paint to resemble oranges, apples, onions (use white paint, adding lines with markers after the paint is dry), and lemons. Form avocados and potatoes by molding the newspaper wads into ovular shapes. Cucumbers, zucchini, and bananas will require the paper wads to be molded into banana shapes. Larger wads of paper can become heads of lettuce or cabbage (use light green paint). Empty toilet paper rolls can be painted yellow and kernels can be drawn on with markers to resemble ears of corn.

Number and operations

- Suggest that children set up a farmers' market to sell the papier-mâché produce, placing their art products in small plastic baskets on a table with the toy cash register and scale. Tell students they need to set prices for their fruit and vegetables and prepare small signs so customers will know the cost. Introduce information about quantity (dozen, half-dozen), price (cost per pound, cost per item), and stocking and restocking the baskets. As customers purchase produce, the sellers will practice their skills counting money and change as they use the toy cash register.

Weighing

- Provide plastic fruit, bags, posters with cost per pound, and scales for weighing the fruit. Students can use the cost per pound to determine the cost of their bag.

Sorting

- Empty seed packets can be sorted by type and placed in a display box for the center.

Reading and computation
- Provide seed catalogues, copies of the order forms from the catalogues (or simplified ones that you have made), and lists of supplies that are needed for the store. Children can find the items in the catalogues, complete an order form, and figure the cost for the order.

Planning and organizational skills
- As students set up their farmers' market, they are using planning and organizational skills.

Other Ideas
- For younger children, teach the well-known songs "Old MacDonald" and "Farmer in the Dell" (and its accompanying game). Place popsicle sticks in the art center and suggest to children that they trace and cut out farm animal stick puppets to make visual aids for the "Old MacDonald" song.
- Bring in produce from the grocery store (or a local farmers' market) and encourage children to make a salad to add to their lunch. Review the process farmers used to grow the food and bring it to market while your group is eating lunch.
- First and second graders can make farm animal sock puppets. Request that families send in slightly used socks and put them in the art center with pieces of felt, yarn, buttons, and large needles and thread for children to design their puppets.
- If you did not prepare a garden with the florist center study (see Chapter 8), you might want to develop a vegetable garden with the children. If space is not available on the playground for a garden, a window box herb garden is another option.
- If you have thought about bringing a pet into the classroom, this study could prompt the addition of a bird or a rabbit. Bird feeders and rabbit hutches are available at farm supply stores.

Book Connections
- Cowley, J. (2006). *Mrs. Wishy Washy's farm*. New York, NY: Puffin.
- Cowley, J. (1999). *The rusty, trusty tractor*. Honesdale, PA: Boyds Mills Press.
- Cronin, D. (2006). *Dooby dooby moo*. New York, NY: Atheneum Press.
- Hutchins, P. (1971). *Rosie's walk*. New York, NY: Aladdin.
- Jones, C. (1998). *Old MacDonald had a farm*. Boston, MA: Sandpiper.

FARM AND FARM SUPPLY CENTER

Items That Families Might Donate or Loan to the Center

- slightly used socks (child- and adult-sized)
- empty food containers
- empty seed packets
- outdated newspapers
- specialized farm supplies

ARCHEOLOGY AND PALEONTOLOGY CENTER

This center can either be an outside center or an inside one. The box can either be made into a cart for carrying all of the tools that the scientists need, or it can be used as part of a museum to display artifacts that have been recovered from the "dig." To make a cart, old wagon or cart wheels can be attached by a metal rod that goes through a hole in the center of each long side of the box. A handle would then be fashioned out of a strip of corrugated cardboard and attached to one of the short sides using brads. To make a display case for a museum, turn the box upside down. Artifacts can be displayed on the box and descriptions of the artifacts can be written on large sticky notes and posted on the sides of the box under the specific artifact.

Plaster of Paris may be used to produce fossils. Plants can be pressed into it and then allowed to harden to produce plant fossils. You can produce dinosaur footprints by pouring the plaster into a meat tray from the grocery store and then making dinosaur tracks using plastic dinosaurs. If there is a museum relatively near your school, contact it to see if it has any loaner materials related to this topic. Some of the larger museums have loaner boxes that contain fossil replicas and other materials on this topic.

To simulate a dig, use the top of the box and place kitty litter, sand, aquarium gravel, or dirt in the box. Hide artifacts in the box lid and cover them with the material you put in the box. A broken saucer, penny with a date from many years ago (such as 1969), and a button might be put in the box. The idea would be that the children will infer that the items are all from around 1969. You can use a box that is about 6 inches deep to set up fossils in different layers for excavation. Layers could be plaster of Paris with an item buried in it (plastic dinosaur), followed by gravel with an arrowhead in it, followed by kitty litter with a rusty bolt, and then the aquarium gravel with a modern-day item.

Contents

- paint brushes of various sizes
- trowels
- some type of screen or sifter
- fossils
- arrowheads (can be replicas)
- coins with dates from several years ago
- broken pottery that can be reassembled
- soil, kitty litter, or aquarium gravel
- graph paper
- pencils
- sticky notes
- rulers
- tape
- string

ARCHEOLOGY AND PALEONTOLOGY CENTER

Content Information

- Explain to the children that an archeologist studies about the history of people, while a paleontologist studies prehistoric life such as dinosaurs and fossils.
- When scientists think they might have a site with artifacts, they will set up a grid and begin digging. They will carefully sift all of the dirt looking for very small artifacts. They use trowels and then small brushes when they find an artifact to uncover it and keep it from being damaged.
- Fossils are animals or plants that have had their bodies or parts replaced with minerals, so they are hard like a rock but still look like the animal or have the impression in a rock of what they looked like.
- The age of artifacts can sometimes be determined by the strata, or level, at which it is found.

Vocabulary Enrichment

- prehistoric
- fossils
- paleontologist
- archeologist
- extinction
- cold blooded
- dinosaurs
- skeleton
- dig
- survey
- excavation
- looting
- fakes
- civilizations
- agriculture
- elite
- aristocrats
- midden
- artifacts
- shards
- test pits
- ground penetrating radar
- grid
- stratigraphy
- strata
- trowels
- sketch

Dramatic Play/Cooperation

- A good place to start when introducing young children to the concept of being an archeologist or paleontologist is through dinosaurs. Young children are very interested in dinosaurs. This would be the starting point for discussing how fossils are extracted from the ground.
- It will be very appealing to the children to get to dig and find artifacts. Proper use of the tools will need to be explained to them. Tell students that the idea isn't to run your hands through and find the artifacts. The idea is to

find them without moving them. This has to be done very carefully. That is why a small brush is used.

Skills

Fine-motor development
- Using the box lid with kitty litter, bury an arrowhead and a few other items in the box. The children will use the small brushes to uncover the items.

Matching
- Using the plaster of Paris footprints, the children can match the fossils to the plastic dinosaurs.

Sketching
- Older or more advanced students can sketch the artifacts that they uncover on graph paper.

Working with grids
- Before the children begin to dig in the box, they can lay out a grid using tape and string. The box would accommodate three strings being placed lengthwise on the lid of the box and four strings widthwise. The children can then use sticky notes to mark A, B, and C, and one, two, three, and four for the sections. When an artifact is found, they can record its location on the sketch (e.g., B2).
- Children can hide artifacts in the grid and write the grid location for others to find.

Writing
- Have the children write information for a museum display about the artifacts that they recovered from their dig.

Reading and research
- If you have many common fossils in the center, add a book on fossil identification and let children attempt to identify the fossils and then research them online.
- Bring in books and magazines that show excavations with a grid laid out and people using the brushes and other tools to uncover the artifacts. Look for websites that show current digs and post those websites by the computer for students to visit.

Other Ideas
- Visit a museum and notice how the artifacts are displayed and what information is provided.

- Provide the children with meat trays and plaster of Paris. Take them outside and let them find a leaf to impress in the plaster. You should pour the plaster into the trays for the students and supervise their use of the plaster.
- Look around the playground after it has rained for animal tracks. Mix up plaster of Paris and pour it into the print. Let it harden and then remove it and show it to the children. They enjoy being a part of the process.
- Learn songs about dinosaurs. Write the words on a large chart and use that as part of reading instruction for the younger children. You can make up your own song using a familiar tune. Here is an example sung to the tune of "The Itsy Bitsy Spider":

  The little baby dinosaur went up the big, big hill.
  Along came T-Rex and chased the baby down.
  Up ran momma dinosaur and chased T-Rex away.
  And the little baby dinosaur went up the big hill again.

  Or this one sung to the tune of "Twinkle, Twinkle, Little Star":

  T-Rex, T-Rex, what do you see?
  I see humans looking at me.
  Dinos used to roam all around,
  Now all that's left are bones to be found.
  T-Rex, T-Rex, what do you see?
  I see humans looking at me.

- A sample dig could even be conducted on the school grounds. Depending upon the school's location, real fossils and/or Indian pottery shards might be found.

Book Connections

- Aliki. (1990). *Fossils tell of long ago.* New York, NY: HarperCollins.
- DK Publishing. (1994). *Big book of dinosaurs.* New York, NY: Author.
- Evert, L. (2004). *Rocks, fossils and arrowheads.* Minneapolis, MN: North-Word.

Items That Families Might Donate or Loan to the Center

- collections of fossils and American Indian artifacts
- small antiques

Chapter 12   **For Fun Centers**

Children and their families look forward to weekends and vacations, because they love opportunities to participate in activities together. The joy in family life is all about planning a weekend picnic, going to a county fair, riding the Ferris wheel with other family members, or visiting a nearby zoo. Going to the beach or taking in a camping trip are the foundation for family memories that last a lifetime.

The learning center boxes described in this chapter are "just for fun." As you plan center activities organized here, find joy in the delight and pleasure children will discover as they learn about amusement parks, zoos, and rodeos. Be prepared to hear about memories they and their families have already made.

CAMPING CENTER

If you plan on using a tent with this center, the classroom must be big enough to have a fairly large area to place it. A tent may also be made by draping a sheet over a rope that is tied between two small posts or even chairs. If a tent is not going to be used, this center can be a backpacking center. The box can be used to simply store the center's pieces, or the box can be turned into a camper's pantry and stove. To make the box into the stove and pantry, place the box on a table and remove the lid. On one of the long sides at both corners, you will need to cut down from the top to the bottom, freeing this side (one open side cut; see Figure 2). Fold the long side out. This will be the cook stove for your camp. Draw two burners on this side. The inside of the box can be for storing all of your cookware, utensils, and food. This space will be the pantry. If you really want to get creative, screw a towel rack on one of the short sides and hang a towel there, or simply hang a small hand towel over the side of the box. Place a bowl beside this for your sink.

For the teacher with a little more money to spend, a two-burner drip pan may be purchased at a home center. This can be placed on the side that folds down. A small rack for kitchen cabinets can also be purchased and used inside the box to divide up the space. Dishes can be placed below, and cans and boxes can be placed above. If you have an army surplus store near you, old mess kits can be purchased for the center.

You will need to decide how involved you are going to make this center. You may find that children are so interested in the topic that you may want to include mountain climbing and its related gear, survival training, forest wildlife identification, orienteering, and fishing. Each of these areas will be briefly touched on in this center, but a teacher should always be prepared to take the children further into a topic in which they show real interest.

Contents

- empty, clean food cans (opening cans from the bottom will increase the realistic look of the cans, and any paper wrappers should be examined to be sure that no food remains that might attract bugs)
- cooking pots, pans, and utensils
- paper plates and plastic cups and silverware
- table cloth
- empty condiment bottles (e.g., mustard, catsup, salt, pepper)
- sleeping bags
- tent
- cook stove or camp stove
- compass
- small fishing pole with a magnet on the end
- cutouts of fish that have been laminated and have a paperclip attached to the nose
- binoculars
- books that identify insects, animals, and birds
- magnifiers
- magnifier boxes (can hold dead insects for the children to identify and examine)

Content Information

- Show all of the equipment that backpackers will place in their packs and explain their purposes.
- Talk about why backpackers might take freeze-dried foods along with them.
- Talk about camp safety and safety in the woods. What should campers do if they get lost?
- Water in creeks and rivers is not safe to drink and must be purified. Tell students the different ways to do this. If you are backpacking, water is heavy and it is not possible to take as much water as you need in your pack.
- Cooking in camp may be over a cook stove that runs from gas in a container, over a fire, or over a backpacking stove. Talk about how this is different from cooking at home and identify some of the problems with preparing a meal this way.
- Campers sleep in tents or under the stars. Think about some problems they might have in doing this (e.g., rain, bugs).

Vocabulary Enrichment

- canteen
- freeze-dried food
- gear
- propane stove
- hydration systems
- water purification
- inflatable
- binoculars
- hatchet
- air mattress
- duffel bags
- sleeping bag
- compass
- GPS system
- map
- contour map
- potable water
- cooler
- Dutch oven
- survival
- reels
- lures

Dramatic Play/Cooperation

- Children will really get involved with dramatic play in this center; the more props you provide, the more enhanced their play.
- Read books to the children about camping experiences so that they can have an understanding of what happens. Many younger children may not have been camping.
- Have books and posters around the room that show different camping scenes.

CAMPING CENTER

CAMPING CENTER

- Guidelines will need to be set with use of a tent. You will have to decide how many students will be allowed in the tent at one time. Also, be sure that your tent is placed so that you can see inside it. This could be a safety issue.

Skills

Tasting

- Let students touch, smell, and taste freeze-dried food. Add water to rehydrate the food and allow them to touch, smell, and taste it this way. Talk about the difference.

Matching upper and lowercase letters

- Use a permanent marker to write uppercase and lowercase letters on the laminated fish. The children can then fish for matches. (The letters can be erased by using hairspray on a tissue. This will allow the teacher to change what is on the fish.)

Rhyming words

- Write rhyming words on the fish and have students fish for matches.

Reading, writing, and planning

- Plan a menu for three meals for three days using the materials that are in the camper's pantry.

Alphabetical order

- Place food items in the pantry in alphabetical order by first letter (younger students) or first and second letter (older or advanced students).

Map skills

- Very young students can be given a simple map of the campsite and shown how a map is a paper representation of a real thing. Older students can be exposed to contour maps and make maps of their own. All of the terms associated with maps, such as compass rose and scale, could be included in a lesson. The camp could be rearranged and the children could draw a map of the new camp.

Finding cardinal directions, following written directions, and writing directions

- With the compass, students can be given a map of the classroom and written directions about how to find a "spring" for water. The map would tell them to start at a certain place and go so many steps north (or in any other direction). When a child finds the spring, which could be represented with a canteen, he will then hide the canteen and write directions for another child.

Observation and research

- Binoculars can be placed beside the classroom window along with a bird identification book. The children can observe the birds through the window with the binoculars and then try to identify them. A clipboard can be kept by the window for the children's notes and sketches. If it is possible, place a bird feeder within viewing from the window and keep seed in it to encourage the birds to come. Students can also graph the type and number of birds that come to the feeder.

- Have muddy water in a tub and a hand pump purification unit. Let the children draw water through the unit and compare the difference with the untreated water.

Using a scale
- Bottles with varying amounts of water can be provided for the children to weigh and record their weight.

Reading a thermometer and weather reports in the paper
- Knowing what the weather is going to be like is important for campers. Reading a thermometer is very difficult for children, so this activity would be best with older students. Have them look at the weather report in a newspaper and decide if they should go camping today. They can make a poster that displays the weather for the day.

Other Ideas

- Bring in different-sized water bottles and have the children predict how much each bottle holds and then actually pour water into the bottles and measure it.
- Invite someone who backpacks to your classroom to talk about what it really is like. Ask him to bring his pack and show your students everything he carries and explain its purpose. Let the children try to lift the pack.
- Use a bow, piece of wood, and a stick and try to start a fire. This obviously will need to be done outside. More than likely, the children will not be able to start the fire, but allow them to feel the heat that is generated when the stick spins against another piece of wood. Stores that sell Boy Scout items will often have a fire starting kit.
- If school policy permits, you can bring in a real camp stove, and the children can help you plan and cook a meal outside.
- Brainstorm ideas about how to survive in different scenarios (e.g., You got lost in the woods and it is getting dark. What should you do?).
- Simple first aid could be introduced during this time.
- Study of the night sky and the constellations would also be appropriate with this center.

Book Connections

- Brunelle, L. (2007). *Camp out! The ultimate kids' guide.* New York, NY: Workman.

CAMPING CENTER

- Mayer, M. (2002). *Camping out.* Grand Rapids, MI: School Specialty Publishing.
- Parish, P. (2003). *Amelia Bedelia goes camping.* New York, NY: HarperCollins.
- Rey, M., &. Rey, H. A. (1999). *Curious George goes camping.* New York, NY: Houghton Mifflin.

Items That Families Might Donate or Loan to the Center

- small dome tent
- canteen
- lantern
- freeze-dried food (some to taste and some empty bags for play)
- backpacks
- contour maps
- ground pad
- sleeping bags
- small backpacking stove without fuel
- backpacking pots and pans
- camp stools and chairs
- camp sink
- cooking utensils
- empty cans and food wrappers

BEACH CENTER

The beach is an enchanting place for children. The box for this center will be a diorama of a beach. With the box flat on the table, cut both ends of one of the long sides from the top down to the bottom. Now continue cutting along the crease of the bottom, freeing both short sides so that they will fold out. The box will now be spread out (three open sides cut; see Figure 3). On the long side that is now flat on the table, glue down sandpaper. This will be the beach. For the water, buy a large piece of blue felt that will cover the bottom of the box and will be large enough to fit under the folded out sides. This is the ocean. Paint the back of the box and the two sides that are folded out with a very light blue colored paint. This will be the sky.

Discount stores, party stores, and stores that stock craft supplies will offer items for this center. Look at party stores for small umbrellas (like those used in drinks) and plastic sea animals. You can also look at the scrapbooking supplies for items that would go on the beach. The idea is for the children to classify items by placing them on the sand, in the water, or in the sky. Laminated pictures can also be used instead of actual items. Items for the sky can be secured by having sticky clay available to hold them on the box. Items for the water and sand can be placed flat on those surfaces. Further interest by the children could result in a study of pirates and treasures, sea creatures, how islands are formed, and other topics.

Contents

- wide variety of different types and sizes of shells
- barnacles
- sea glass (the glass you find on the shore that is worn smooth by the waves and sand)
- driftwood
- shark's teeth or jaws (children should not have free access to the shark's teeth as the teeth can cut them)
- buckets, shovels, towels and blankets, sunscreen, sunglasses, and goggles (for dramatic play)

Content Information

- How much content you provide will depend upon the children's experiences. Children who live relatively near a beach can just have the materials turned over to them. For children who have no concept of a beach, it is very difficult for them to picture sand and water as far as they can see. Taking children outside and asking them to look left, right, and in front of them, picturing being able to see only sand and water might help.
- If the school has a sandbox, the children can lay on a towel and close their eyes, and you can play ocean sounds for them.
- Sunscreen is very important at the beach to protect your skin.

- People can build sandcastles and other sculptures at the beach, but if you build them too close to the water, the tide coming in will wash it away. The erosion tub could show this.
- Shells had animals that lived in them.
- Waves can be weak or strong enough to knock you over. They can also be very small or very tall.

Vocabulary Enrichment

- seashore
- shells
- sandcastles
- sculptures
- barnacles
- spiral (shell description)
- shore
- jetty
- mariners
- tideland
- tides
- waves
- ocean
- sea
- lake

- dunes
- drift line
- deposition
- erosion
- tsunami
- coral reef
- artificial reefs
- sand
- driftwood
- artificial beaches
- pier
- surf
- shorebirds
- sea turtles
- beach habitats

Dramatic Play/Cooperation

- A large piece of blue and brown butcher paper could be spread on the floor to represent the beach and the water. The children can use the dolls and beach items for their day at the beach. A picnic basket can be added with play food.
- Different sizes of boxes covered in brown paper can be use for building sand castles.

Skills

Sorting

- With a large supply of shells, the children can sort them by shell type, shell size, color, smoothness, or ones with ridges.

Sequencing a story

- Provide books such as *A Chance for Esperanza* (Schiller & Ada, 1997). Read the book and have pictures for the younger children to place in the sequence of events in the story. Older children can be provided with descriptive paragraphs to read and properly sequence.

Word problems with addition and subtraction

- Students can be given shells to use as manipulatives in figuring out word problems. Laminate the problems and have a dry erase marker for the children to use to answer the problems. This activity can be made self-correcting by placing the answer on the back under a flap (to discourage casual looking).

Classification

- Younger children can be given a doll with many accessories and clothes. They have to pack the beach bag with the appropriate items. Laminated paper items could be used.
- Older children can be given laminated paper mammals and fish that live in the ocean. They can separate them on a laminated ocean.

Understanding erosion

- In a clean plastic tub, make a slanted beach across the bottom and up one side out of sand. Carefully add water, being sure you keep a good part of the beach dry. Show the students how to carefully make waves with their hands. Observe what happens. The children can then sketch and write about erosion.

Measuring

- Have the children measure a 15-meter (50 feet) tsunami by measuring yarn in the classroom. Take them outside and lay out the yarn on the playground. Have a child stand at each end to give students some idea how big that is. Find a tree or something that they can see that is about 50-feet high. The largest recorded tsunami was in Alaska in 1958. It was 1,700 feet tall.
- Have tall containers of water available and a piece of string that has knots every inch and a small fishing sinker at the bottom. Have students measure the water depth by using the string and counting the knots. Knotted ropes have been used for many years by mariners to measure water depth.
- Give children a 6-foot length of rope (or yarn) and have them make a knot every foot. Have students measure each other and things in the classroom and record the length.

Legends and myths

- Show the children a sand dollar and explain to them the legend of the sand dollar. Talk about what legends are. Ask them if they know of any legends. Have them write a legend of their own to share with the class.
- Discuss the myths of sea monsters and mermaids. Talk about what things in real life could be mistaken for such creatures.

Using technology
- Have the children choose an animal that lives in or by the sea. They will then use the computer to find out information about this animal, write a report, spell check it, and print it for sharing with others.

Other Ideas
- Have the children make a large mural that shows what they have learned about the beach. It can include animals in the water, on the beach, and in the air. Older children can write description of processes such as wave action.
- Discuss beach safety. Everything from sunscreen to undertow can be part of this lesson.
- Focus on the different jobs that involve the beach and sea. Short sections of TV shows featuring fishing, policing, underwater exploration, and other jobs can be shown as a way to give students more understanding of what these jobs would be like.
- Bring sand, buckets of water, and various containers to the playground and let children build sandcastles. Be sure to let the parents know what you are doing so they can dress their children appropriately.
- A tsunami moves at a speed of 600 mph, or 60 feet per second. Take the children out on the playground and ask them if they think they can outrun a tsunami. Have a marker 60 feet away and tell students they need to race to this marker. Tell them the tsunami is one mile away and give them some visual idea about how far away it is. Then, give them 6 seconds to run before yelling "stop."

Book Connections
- Mayer, M. (2003). *Beach day*. Greensboro, NC: Carson-Dellosa.
- Rey, H. A. (1999). *Curious George goes to the beach*. New York, NY: Houghton Mifflin.
- Rockwell, A., & Rockwell, H. (1991). *At the beach*. New York, NY: Aladdin.
- Roosa, K. (2001). *Beach day*. New York, NY: Clarion.
- Schiller, P., & Ada, A. F. (1997). *A chance for Esperanza*. Columbus, OH: McGraw-Hill.

Items That Families Might Donate or Loan to the Center
- shells
- shark's teeth and jaws
- dried starfish
- sand dollars
- sea glass

AMUSEMENT PARK CENTER

Your decision to plan an amusement park center depends on the availability of park options in your area. You may want to label your study as a circus or carnival center. Many communities host annual county fairs that attract carnival rides, which travel on a circuit from town to town. If you are aware that the carnival is coming to town, begin your amusement park study.

Use the amusement park box to prepare a ticket stand. You can paint stripes along the sides of the box and on the lid or you can use red masking tape to position stripes on the box. Write the word *Tickets* on a piece of poster board and affix the label on one side of the box. Many of the activities described here imply that the amusement park will be on the playground. The ticket box can be moved wherever you plan for the center to be located. When using it in your classroom, position the box near your dramatic play center.

Contents

- travel brochures that describe area amusement and theme parks
- costumes that represent figures children will have seen during visits to amusement parks (e.g., clowns, princesses, Disney or cartoon characters)
- Velcro dartboard
- ball or beanbag toss game
- deflated swimming pool
- bowling pins
- rolls of tickets
- teacher-prepared clown shoe patterns
- balls of various sizes
- photographs of Ferris wheels, rollers coasters, merry-go-rounds, and circus tents

Content Information

- Talk to children about an amusement park you have visited and show them photographs of your adventure. Ask them to tell about their experiences with amusement parks.
- Discuss the variety of carnival rides that are available at amusements parks and the jobs that carnival workers perform. Tell students that carnival workers often travel from town to town, transporting all of the equipment they need in moving vans and large trucks. Their jobs include setting up the equipment and taking it down, running the machinery, and making sure that it is safe for their customers.

AMUSEMENT PARK CENTER

AMUSEMENT PARK CENTER

Vocabulary Enrichment

- amusement park
- amusement
- amuse
- theme park
- carnival
- carnival rides
- Ferris wheels
- merry-go-round
- bumper cars
- roller coasters
- main gate
- vendors
- ticket seller
- big tent
- county fair
- costumes

Dramatic Play/Cooperation

- Add several new costumes to your usual dramatic play area to encourage amusement park play. Clown suits and masks, capes, a ballet costume, a top hat, sequined jackets or vests, pairs of white or black gloves, suspenders, wigs of all colors, and oversized shirts and slacks are suitable for developing amusement park play. Disney and princess costumes create enthusiastic responses from students. Hula hoops, wands, lion tamer whips, and a roll of tickets are beneficial for promoting play experiences.

Skills

Fine-motor development
- Introduce juggling skills to children. Begin by juggling one ball, then two balls, then three.
- Allow children to play darts with the Velcro dartboard to improve aim.

Gross-motor development
- Use a child's bowling game so children can practice their skill at throwing balls.

Knowing personal information
- When you provide children opportunities to use the amusement park obstacle course, using play money for ticket purchases is great for helping students recognizing coin values. But you might want to ask for personal information from students as the purchase price for participation. Here are some suggestions to use at various times (or with specific students):
  o Tell me your phone number.
  o Tell your home address.
  o What is your whole name?
  o Where do your parents (or guardians) work?
  o How do you get in touch with your parents (or guardians)?

- If children perform well with their answers, challenge them by asking for cognitive information, such as:
  - o Write your first name.
  - o Name these shapes (show two or three).
  - o What is this color (show samples of various colored paper)?
  - o Name this alphabet letter.
  - o Match this lowercase letter with its uppercase letter.
  - o Tell me a word that starts with (name a consonant).

Parts of speech
- After reading *Merry-Go-Round: A Book About Nouns* (Heller, 1998) to your second-grade class, define nouns as words that name objects. Consult your classroom word wall to count the number of nouns that are on the board. If they understand this information easily, introduce children to verbs, prepositions, and conjunctions.

Writing
- Children in second grade can do Internet searches to conduct research on the history of Ferris wheels, roller coasters, carousels, and theme parks. If this project is done with small groups of children, they can write a report to share with their peers or with other second graders in the school. Consider asking them to prepare models or poster board visual aids to enhance their reports.

Estimation and weighing
- Have toy trucks marked with the amount of weight (load) that each truck can handle. Prepare small bags of varying weights. Let students estimate how many bags each truck can carry and then check their estimates using a postal scale.

Counting money
- Have items (e.g., popcorn, cotton candy, peanuts, sodas) for sale at the concession stand. Children will pick up a small purse or wallet, count the money inside, and use the play money inside to make their purchases.

Other Ideas

- Younger groups of students will enjoy a ball pool experience. Inflate a plastic pool and place many colorful balls in it. Children can roll around in the balls or toss the balls into the pool. As a challenge, ask them to separate the balls into piles of specific colors or count the balls.
- Plan an obstacle course on the playground or in the gym to represent an amusement park for your classroom. Organize so that children:
  - o somersault or log roll on tumbling mats,

AMUSEMENT PARK CENTER

o   slither through a plastic tunnel,

o   slide down the playground slide,

o   crawl under or climb over sawhorses,

o   run around barrels,

o   jump through hula hoops, and/or

o   wade through a plastic inflatable pool filled with balls.

- Provide crepe paper so children can fashion large clown collars to wear around their necks.

- Make clown hats by forming large pieces of construction paper into cones and trimming excess paper and gluing (or stapling) the paper edges into place. Students can decorate these with stickers or use markers to make interesting designs. The hats should be large enough to place on their heads without slipping.

- Trace and enlarge a pair of adult shoes onto poster board and cut them out. Trace circles in the heel of the shoe pattern, cut out the circles, and clip a slit at the back of the shoe pattern. Provide colored construction paper and ask children to trace the patterns and cut them out to use as clown shoes, which they slip over their own shoes. They can also decorate the shoes if they want prior to putting them on as clown shoes.

- Use the familiar "Hokey Pokey" song to lead children in a hokey pokey clown song when they are wearing their clown shoes. Just for fun, paint children's noses red (if they wish) and ask them to wear their clown collars when you sing the song. Add verses about their collars and noses.

    You put your big shoe in, you take your big shoe out;
    You put your big shoe in and shake it all about.
    Do the hokey pokey and turn yourself around;
    That's what it's all about!

- Invite a family volunteer into the classroom to do face painting as a special treat for children. Card and party shops often sell stickers and stamps that can serve as face painting facsimiles if this an approach you would prefer.

- If you did not use the art car parade activity described in the car care center, use the instructions for making art cars to make bumper car boxes for students' play during the amusement park study. Children should be in charge of decorating the cars if they wish.

- If you set aside a special amusement park celebration date, invite local vendors to come in and provide cotton candy, snow cones, and popcorn for students' consumption. One of your families may be helpful in funding this request or coordinate your efforts with other teachers in the school to minimize the cost of this event. A high school booster club or other organization may be able to loan you these machines or offer to donate their time making the treats. Children should be able to use lemonade packets to make drinks for the occasion.

- Locate a cardboard cutout of a clown or an amusement park figure that has an opening positioned so that you can take photographs of children with their heads poking through the hole. These standup cutouts are available at many card and party shops, but you can also find them online at a reasonable price. One of your creative family member volunteers might be able to make one of these for you if you send out a request.

Book Connections

- Heller, R. (1998). *Merry-go-round: A book about nouns.* New York, NY: Putnam Juvenile.
- Horvath, P. (1999). *When the circus came to town.* New York, NY: Farrar, Straus & Giroux.

Items That Families Might Donate or Loan to the Center

- photographs of their trips to parks (with their names on the back of each) or brochures about the parks they have visited
- costumes
- small balls or beanbags
- a roll of tickets
- volunteer time or services making popcorn, snow cones, or cotton candy

AMUSEMENT PARK CENTER

 **ZOO CENTER**

Decorating your zoo center box is optional; but if you want to decorate it, begin by tracing animal stencils on each of the four sides of the box. Then vertically align strips of brown or black construction paper on top of the animal drawings to resemble the bars on an animal's cage. Spray the box with an enamel sealant or place contact paper on each side to prolong the life of the box. The lid can be painted to match the construction paper bars and appear to be the roof of the cage. The completed box will not be needed for many of the activities described for this center, other than serving as a focus for the children about the nature of the zoo study that will continue for several days. Your children may want to use it during their dramatic play, so have it available for easy access by youngsters.

You will want to visit the San Diego Zoo website to acquire a wealth of knowledge for yourself about zoos and zoo life. The site includes a section titled "Animal Bytes," which shares information about animal categories, their countries of origin, animal group names, and their scientific names. The zoo has live Panda Cam, Polar Cam, Ape Cam, and Elephant Cam options and videos that allow viewers to see numerous animals housed in its habitats. Each cam site provides fun facts about specific animals, their habitats and ecosystems, and information about animal conservation programs for endangered species.

Contents

- at least one set of zoo animal figures (available for purchase at most teacher supply stores)
- copies of *Ranger Rick, Your Big Backyard, National Wildlife, Animal Baby,* and other scientific journals or magazines that feature photographs of exotic animals, or sets of greeting cards, calendars, and posters purchased from National Wildlife Federation
- zoo animal stencils
- set of animal photograph cards
- world map
- jungle helmet, white or khaki shirt, white or khaki pair of pants, and a pair of walking boots (to allow a child to transform himself into an animal trainer or a safari tour guide)
- zoo animal costumes and masks

Content Information

- Talk to children about zoos. Ask if they know the reasons zoos exist. Give them a chance to talk about a zoo they may have visited.
- Tell students that most zoos house animals that are not native to the United States. Tell them that most zoo animals live in jungles, deserts, or grass-

ZOO CENTER

lands in foreign countries before they are brought to the zoo to live. Show photographs of these natural habitats.

- Define the categories of animals that visitors will see when they visit zoos: amphibians, birds, mammals, and reptiles. Larger zoos may also have insect exhibits. Tell children that these animals are classified by their diet: *carnivores* (animals that are meat eaters), *herbivores* (animals that eat plants), and *insectivores* (those that eat insects).

- Introduce the word *safari* to children and describe what happens during a safari. If one of your students' family members has ever taken an African safari, extend an invitation for that person to visit the classroom and share information with your group.

Vocabulary Enrichment

- lion
- elephant
- giraffe
- rhinoceros
- hippopotamus
- monkey
- chimpanzee
- ape
- gorilla
- tiger
- cheetah
- jaguar
- puma
- big cat
- bear

- panda
- koala
- eucalyptus
- bamboo
- natural habitat
- carnivore
- herbivore
- insectivore
- predator
- safari
- exhibit
- display
- zookeeper
- caretaker

Dramatic Play/Cooperation

- Animal costumes and masks will enhance dramatic play opportunities. Some children may pretend to be animal trainers once this job has been defined.

- Most of the time, children will enjoy playing with the zoo animal figures you have stored in the box. They will make up stories about the animals and their imitations of the sounds animals make will provide a delightful classroom experience.

- After learning what a safari is, encourage students to take a safari around the classroom looking for animals you have hidden. If your school is small,

ZOO CENTER

ZOO CENTER

you might hide animals in various spots around the building and the playground to expand the safari experience.

Skills

Positional words

- Place zoo animal figures around the room. Then give individual children instructions for find specific selections:
  o Find the gorilla *on top of* the cubbies.
  o Find the rhinoceros *behind* the wastebasket.
  o Find the lion *beside* the classroom door.
  o Find the panda *under* the snack table.
  o Find the elephant *in front of* the bulletin board.

Reading positional words

- Write the above sentences on index cards for children to read and find the animals.

Listening to riddles

- Place the zoo animal figures around the classroom. Describe various characteristics of animals and ask individual students to find each one (e.g., I'm thinking of an animal that roars, has a lot of hair around its head called a *mane*, and is called the king of the jungle).

Tracing

- Place zoo animal stencils in the art center, so children can trace and cut out their creations. Display their efforts on a classroom bulletin board and label it as "Our Class Zoo." If this is an open-ended activity, children can return as many times as they wish to cut out additional animals.

Matching

- Using Tessa Paul's (1998) *In the Jungle* as a guide, prepare a set of animal tracks on index cards and laminate. Ask students to match animal tracks to a photograph of the animal. (*Note:* An Animal Photo Card Library is available for purchase from Lakeshore Learning Materials.)

Classification

- Using a set of animal photographs, ask children to separate animals into three categories: *carnivores*, *herbivores*, and *insectivores*. Classifying animals in this way will require some research on animal diets.

Other Ideas

- Bring a eucalyptus plant to your classroom and talk to children about the koala's diet. Tell children about the medicinal component of eucalyptus.

- For first and second graders, prepare a word scramble indicating that the animals can be found in a zoo (e.g., *etrtul* [*turtle*], *zhpeecimna* [*chimpanzee*], *liaglroat* [*alligator*]).
- Second graders can participate in Internet research about various zoo animals. They can work alone if they are independent learners, but you can also ask students to work in small groups. Request that they find information about the animal's country of origin, its habitat, and the type of food it eats.
- Children can use shoeboxes to prepare animal cages by using markers to resemble bars or by gluing strips of construction paper onto the side of the boxes. Ask them to mold animals with play dough to put inside their boxes.
- Second graders should be able to create acrostics using zoo animal names. Demonstrate how to write an acrostic and challenge them to write their own. Here is an example:

  P arrots
  A re
  g R eat
  bi R ds
  f O r
  T alking

- Play a CD (a good selection is the *The Lion King* soundtrack) and encourage children to move around a large area in the classroom imitating animal movements.
- When using a transition from circle time to center time, ask individual children to move like certain animals.

Book Connections
- Hendrick, M. (1996). *If anything ever goes wrong at the zoo*. Boston, MA: Sandpiper.
- Paul, T. (1998). *In the jungle: Animal trackers around the world*. New York, NY: Crabtree.
- Rose, D. L. (2002). *Birthday zoo*. Morton Grove, IL: Albert Whitman.
- Ryder, J. (2004). *Little panda*. New York, NY: Simon & Schuster.
- Wilson, K. (2004). *Never ever shout at the zoo*. New York, NY: Little, Brown.

That Families Might Donate or Loan to the Center

- animal costumes
- animal photographs
- unused journals or magazines that feature exotic animals

ZOO CENTER

RODEO CENTER

Paint your rodeo center box and the lid with light brown or sand-colored paint. Fashion a dark brown construction paper corral and glue it around all of the sides. The corral fence posts and crossties should be laminated for durability. Add cacti or sagebrush for a creative touch, cut from construction paper or drawn onto the side of the box with markers.

Place the rodeo center near the block center. Use blocks to construct a corral for cattle. If you can locate a rocking horse, add it to promote dramatic play. If it is possible to bring in a saddle and a bale of hay, put the hay in the center and place the saddle on top of it. Children can "ride" the hay bale horse. Some children are allergic to hay, so check your allergy reports prior to bringing hay into the room.

Contents

- cowboy and cattle figurines
- bedroll
- cowboy clothing (e.g., hat, chaps, kerchief, vest, cowboy shirt, jeans, boots)
- CD of western music
- rope
- small tree branches and red cellophane (to allow children to build a pretend campfire)
- pictures of trail drives

Content Information

- Provide basic information about trail rides. When cowboys were hired, they traveled across huge sections of the United States on horseback to round up stray cattle. The cattle trail was long, hot, and dusty, and cowboys spent several weeks doing their jobs. Sometimes they became saddle sore because of the work they did on the trail.
- When they stopped at night, the cook (or "cookie") prepared a meal over a campfire. Cookie clanged a large triangle to call the men to eat. After their evening meal, they would sit around the campfire, tell stories, and sing songs to pass time. Cowboys slept on bedrolls and their saddles served as pillows. Several men watched the herd at night, taking different shifts throughout the night.
- Tell children about the function of cowboy clothing. Cowboy hats protected their heads from the sun. Chaps and jeans protected their legs from cactus plants. Their kerchiefs covered their mouths and noses during dust storms. Cowboys carried knives and other tools in their vests and in saddlebags. They also tied their bedrolls to their saddles so as not to lose them. Boots were essential for protection from venomous snakes.

RODEO CENTER

- If cowboys were rounding up cattle to take to a ranch, they would spend time branding the cattle to show proof of ownership.
- When they finally arrived at their destinations, the men were ecstatic about their jobs being over, and they usually developed an event called a rodeo to celebrate their achievements and demonstrate their skills. They also often participated in square dancing.
- Currently, rodeos usually include steer wrestling, bronco riding, calf roping, team roping, bareback riding, and bull riding competitions. A rodeo event designed specifically for cowgirls is barrel racing. On the pro rodeo circuit, cowgirls and cowboys are given points for their participation in various events and prizes are awarded at the end of the rodeo. Occasionally, belt buckles crafted from silver are given as prizes.
- Describe the role of the rodeo clown to your **students**. He distracts angry animals away from cowboys who may have been thrown off during competitions. The animals chase the clown, who ducks into protective barrels positioned in the rodeo arena while the fallen cowboy is rescued from the arena.

Vocabulary Enrichment

- cowboy
- cowgirl
- trail boss
- trail ride
- night watch
- cook/cookie
- chuck wagon
- tenderfoot
- bedroll (sleeping bag)
- saddle
- reins
- stirrups
- cinch

- boots
- kerchief
- round up
- rope
- lariat
- ukulele
- corral
- cattle brands
- rodeo events
- rodeo arena
- square dancing
- western songs

Dramatic Play/Cooperation

- The block center corral and the contents of the rodeo box should engender rodeo play. If you cannot locate a rocking horse, purchase commercial stick horses or prepare teacher-made versions to place near the center. If the "riding" activity is too rambunctious for indoor play, move the rodeo center outdoors to the playground.

RODEO CENTER

Skills

Gross-motor movement

- Select an identifying spot on the playground for children to run to in a game called stampede. At a given signal, children should run as fast as they can to the appointed goal. The aim of the game is not to win, but to achieve competence with running.
- Place hula hoops approximately 20 feet apart on the playground. Individual students will pretend to be barrel racers, running from the start line in a triangular pattern around each hoop and back to the starting point.

Writing

- Place a chart of words pertinent to trail rides near the writing center for children to refer to when they write stories about the rodeo. Here are a few words to use: *trail ride, trail boss, cookie, chuck wagon, chuck, chili peppers, chili,* and *tenderfoot.*
- Share information about cattle brands and why they were used. Challenge students to develop their own personal cattle brands representing the ranch they might own. The Internet offers information about popular brands cattlemen have used through the years.

Reading and following instructions

- Provide ingredients for trail mix and written instructions for making the mix (e.g., Put two tablespoons of raisins into one of the small cups).
- Provide a plastic plate, pictures of trail-type foods, and cards with varying menus. Children will read the menu and place the food on the plate.

Map skills

- Provide a United States map and information about cattle drives. Children will use the information and find where the cattle drives began and ended.

Other Ideas

- Use the traditional "Going on a Bear Hunt" chant as a model for reviewing what happens during trail rides:

  We're going on a trail ride, going on a trail ride;

  We're not afraid; we're not afraid;

  Got my horse and my rope; got my horse and my rope;

  Giddy up, horse; here we go;

  Uh, oh, what do we see? What do we see?

  It's a wild, raging river, a wild raging river;

  Can't go over it, can't go over it;

  Can't go under it, can't go under it;

  Can't go around it, can't go around it;

  Got to go through it, got to go through it (pretend to swim);

Splash, splash, splash;
Splash, splash, splash.
We're going on a trail ride, going on a trail ride;
We're not afraid; we're not afraid;
Got my horse and my rope; got my horse and my rope;
Giddy up, horse; here we go;
Uh, oh, what do we see? What do we see?
It's a really huge dust storm, really huge dust storm;
Can't go over it, can't go over it;
Can't go under it, can't go under it;
Can't go around it, can't go around it;
Got to go through it, got to go through it (cover noses and mouths).
Cough, cough, cough;
Cough, cough, cough.
We're going on a trail ride, going on a trail ride;
We're not afraid; we're not afraid;
Got my horse and my rope; got my horse and my rope;
Giddy up, horse; here we go;
Uh, oh, what do we see? What do we see?
It's stickly, prickly cactus; stickly, prickly cactus;
Can't go over it, can't go over it;
Can't go under it, can't go under it;
Can't go around it, can't go around it;
Got to go through it, got to go through it (walk gingerly).
Ouch, ouch, ouch;
Ouch, ouch, ouch.
We're going on a trail ride, going on a trail ride;
We're not afraid; we're not afraid;
Got my horse and my rope; got my horse and my rope;
Giddy up, horse; here we go;
Uh, oh, what do we see? What do we see?
It's a huge wet rainstorm, a huge wet rainstorm;
Can't go over it, can't go over it;
Can't go under it, can't go under it;
Can't go around it, can't go around it;
Got to go through it, got to go through it (cover heads);
Watch for raindrops;
Watch for raindrops.
We're going on a trail ride, going on a trail ride;
We're not afraid; we're not afraid;
Got my horse and my rope; got my horse and my rope.

RODEO CENTER

RODEO CENTER

Giddy up, horse; here we go;
Uh, oh, what do we see? What do we see?
It's a great, big cow town; a great, big cow town!
Hey, let's rodeo! Let's rodeo!
We're going to have a hoedown,
We're going to have a hoedown!
Time for fun!

- Prepare cowboy stew for lunch sometime during the rodeo study. Cook stew meat at home and bring it to school in a crockpot. Children can bring vegetables (e.g., beans, corn, canned tomatoes, barley, rice) to put into the stew. Serve the stew with sourdough bread purchased from the grocery store.
- Invite a volunteer to the classroom who can teach children some simple rope tricks. Individuals who participate in professional rodeos also can share information about different rodeo events.

Book Connections
- Brett, J. (1994). *Armadillo rodeo.* New York, NY: Puffin.
- Knowlton, L. L. (1997). *Why cowboys sleep with their boots on.* Gretna, LA: Pelican.

Items That Families Might Donate or Loan to the Center
- sleeping bag
- cowboy clothing
- rope
- pictures of rodeos
- volunteer time teaching rope tricks

Glossary

Beginning sounds: initial phonemes (consonants or vowels) in words.

Classifying: putting objects into categories based on characteristics and attributes (e.g., all red triangles).

Cognitive development: how learners acquire knowledge through experience and growth.

Comparing: viewing at least two objects to determine how they are alike and/or different.

Content knowledge: learners' acquisition of information based on experiences with objects in their environment and interactions with others.

Counting: determining the existence of objects by describing how many there are (referred to as *rational counting; rote counting* is naming numerals from memory).

Dramatic play: taking on roles of adults and animals as part of children's spontaneous activity.

Environmental print: letters and numerals appearing in the environment in deliberate forms (e.g., names of business, traffic signals, signs).

Environmental print album: a collection of print materials put into book form resembling a photograph album.

Environmental scan: a data collection technique (through surveys and interviews) to determine the status of the community in relationship to specific topics.

Estimating: determining and predicting an amount without counting.

Graphing: collecting data and organizing it into a visual display.

Initial consonant sounds: beginning consonant sounds (e.g., /b/ as in *bat*).

Interpretive responses: reactions to classroom experiences through self-expressive activities (e.g., movement, song, artwork, writing).

K-W-L strategy: a teaching strategy used during a thematic study to determine what children know prior to the study (K), what they want to know during the study (W), and what they have learned when the study is completed (L).

Language experience activity: a teaching strategy that allows children to use the language they know to dictate information to adults to put into written form.

Literacy development: experiences young children have that allow them to acquire information about print.

Matching: placing objects together that have common characteristics and attributes.

Mathematical principles: children's understanding of mathematics that serves as a foundation for mathematical skills they will learn later.

Measuring: using standard and nonstandard units to determine size, weight, area, and volume.

Number words: written descriptions of objects (referred to as *numerals*).

One-to-one correspondence: equal matching of one object to another object.

Ordering: placing objects into a specific pattern based on characteristics and attributes.

Pairing: placing two objects together that have common uses.

Prewriting activities: young children's early literacy experiences that resemble writing; sometimes referred to as *scribbles* or *invented spelling*.

Rational counting (see *Counting*)

Rote counting (see *Counting*)

Reading readiness: skills indicating children's ability for learning how to read (awareness of print, recognition of alphabet letters, understanding alphabetic principle).

Repeated addition: a strategy teachers use with young children to build a foundation for understanding multiplication; adding the same number over and over again (4 + 4 + 4 + 4 + 4).

Scientific observation: one of the steps scientists use in the scientific process; children use this process, too, when they learn about organisms and environmental events.

Scientific process: procedures scientists use to prove an hypothesis (i.e., forming an hypothesis, testing the hypothesis through observation and analysis of facts, forming a conclusion).

Sorting: placing objects into categories based on an established criteria (e.g., all items that are the same color).

Story sequence: retelling components of stories in chronological order.

Visual representation: showing information through drawings and displays.

Wheeled toys: large classroom toys that have wheels; children can maneuver them around the classroom or playground with physical movement.

Word wall: a classroom display that lists words children are learning as they participate in early reading and writing activities.

References

Albrecht, K., & Miller, L. (2004). *The comprehensive preschool curriculum*. Beltsville, MD: Gryphon House.

American Association for Gifted Children. (1999). *Characteristics and traits of a gifted preschooler*. Retrieved from http://www.education.com/reference/article/Ref_Testing

American Association for Gifted Children. (2010). *Project Bright IDEA 2: Interest Development Early Abilities 2004–2009*. Retrieved from http://www.aagc.org.

Bodrova, E., & Leong, D. (2007). *Tools of the mind: The Vygotskian approach to early childhood education*. Upper Saddle River, NJ: Pearson/Merrill Prentice Hall.

Byrnes, J. (2001). *Cognitive development and learning in instructional contexts* (2nd ed.). Boston, MA: Allyn & Bacon.

Centers for Disease Control and Prevention. (2009). *Prevalence of autism spectrum disorders—Autism and developmental disabilities monitoring network, United States, 2006*. Retrieved from http://www.cdc.gov/mmwr/preview/mmwrhtml/ss5810a1.htm

Elementary and Secondary Education Act.§ 207, 70 U.S.C. § 7801. 1988.

Gardner, H. (2003, April 21). *Multiple intelligences after twenty years*. Paper presented at the American Educational Research Association, Chicago, Illinois. Retrieved from http://www.pz.harvarded/PIs/HG_MI_after20_years.pdf

Gestwicki, C. (1999). *Developmentally appropriate practice: Curriculum and development in early education* (2nd ed.). Albany, NY: Delmar.

Heller, R. (1998). *Merry-go-round: A book about nouns*. New York, NY: Putnam Juvenile.

Hyson, M. (2008). *Enthusiastic and engaged learners*. New York, NY: Teachers College Press.

Katz, L., & Chard, S. (2000). *Engaging children's minds: The project approach*. Stamford, CT: Ablex.

McAfee, O., & Leong, D. (2002). *Assessing and guiding young children's development and learning.* Boston, MA: Allyn & Bacon.

McLaughlin, B. (1995). *Fostering second language development in young children: Principles and practices.* Retrieved from http://repositories.cdlib.org/crede/ncrcdslleducational/EPR14

National Association for the Education of Young Children. (2009). *Where we stand on responding to linguistic and cultural diversity.* Retrieved from http://www.naeyc.org/ files/naeyc/file/positions/diversity.pdf

National Association for the Education of Young Children, & National Association of Early Childhood Specialists in State Departments of Education. (2003). *Early childhood curriculum, assessment, and program evaluation—Building an effective, accountable system in programs for children birth through age 8.* Retrieved from http://www.naeyc.org/files/naeyc/file/positions/pscape.pdf

National Association for Gifted Children. (2010). *Jacob Javits Gifted and Talented Students Education Act.* Retrieved from http://www.nagc.org/index2.aspx?id=572&terms=javits

National Dissemination Center for Children with Disabilities. (2009a). *Attention-deficit/hyperactivity disorder.* Retrieved from http://www.nichcy.org/Disabilities/Specific/Pages/ADHD.aspx

National Dissemination Center for Children with Disabilities. (2009b). *Autism.* Retrieved from http://www.nichcy.org/Disabilities/Specific/Pages/Autism.aspx

National Dissemination Center for Children with Disabilities. (2009c). *Developmental delay.* Retrieved from http://www.nichcy.org/Disabilities/Specific/Pages/DevelopmentalDelay(DD).aspx

National Dissemination Center for Children with Disabilities. (2009d). *Speech and language impairments.* Retrieved from http://www.nichcy.org/Disabilities/Specific/Pages/SpeechLanguageImpairments.aspx

National Dissemination Center for Children with Disabilities. (2009e). *Visual impairments.* Retrieved from http://www.nichcy.org/Disabilities/Specific/Pages/VisualImpairment.aspx

Paul, T. (1998). *In the jungle: Animal trackers around the world.* New York, NY: Crabtree.

Schiller, R., & Ada, A. F. (1997). *A chance for Esperanza.* Columbus, OH: McGraw-Hill.

Taylor, R. (2003). *Assessment of exceptional students: Educational and psychological procedures* (6th ed.). Boston, MA: Pearson.

Warner, L., & Sower, J. (2005). *Educating young children from preschool through primary grades.* Boston, MA: Allyn & Bacon.

Zigler, E., Singer, D., & Bishop-Josef, S. (2004). *Children's play: The roots of reading.* Washington, DC: Zero to Three.

Appendix A

Blank Classroom Data Form

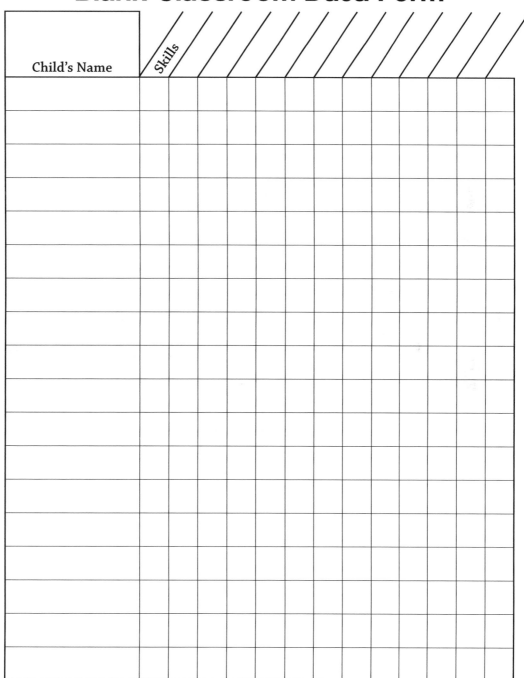

Child's Name	Skills										

Appendix B

Individual Child Assessment Sheet

Name: _____ School Year: _____

Skills	Date Tested/Comments:		

Appendix C

Salt Dough Recipe

Ingredients: 3 cups of flour (not self-rising), 2 cups of salt, 1 ½ cups hot tap water

Directions: Mix ingredients together. Form the shapes that you desire. Food coloring may be added to the dough. Bake your shapes at 325 degrees until done. For thick items, this could be as long as 2–3 hours. You will know that your shapes are done when they are very hard. Allow them to cool completely before painting. Do not store in an airtight container for several weeks. This will allow any moisture that remains to dry. If your shapes are spongy, you still have moisture in them.

About the Authors

Judith Sower has 18 years of teaching experience in public schools. She has taught in inclusive classrooms with many children who had special needs, from those who were gifted and talented to those with disabilities. Her experience includes teaching first, second, and third grades, plus 12 years as a special education teacher with children in kindergarten to sixth grade. She was recognized as Teacher of the Year in Birdville ISD in Texas in 1987. In addition, Judith has taught for 11 years at Sam Houston State University, where she has instructed early childhood and special education courses. She is currently a member of the National Association for the Education of Young Children.

Laverne Warner is Professor Emerita in the Department of Language, Literacy, and Special Populations at Sam Houston State University (SHSU). Her work includes 9 years public school teaching experience, 32 years at SHSU, serving as past president of the Texas Association for the Education of Young Children (TAEYC), advocating for young children, and authoring numerous books and articles about teaching young children. She was named as the Teacher Educator of the Year for TAEYC and received the Excellence in Teaching Award at SHSU in 1992.